Speak Good News

Equipping the Church to Engage
in More Spiritual Conversations

DAVID SCHAAL

Foreword by Kevin G. Harney

WIPF & STOCK · Eugene, Oregon

SPEAK GOOD NEWS
Equipping the Church to Engage in More Spiritual Conversations

Copyright © 2024 David Schaal. All rights reserved. Except for brief quotations in critical publications or reviews, no part of this book may be reproduced in any manner without prior written permission from the publisher. Write: Permissions, Wipf and Stock Publishers, 199 W. 8th Ave., Suite 3, Eugene, OR 97401.

Wipf & Stock
An Imprint of Wipf and Stock Publishers
199 W. 8th Ave., Suite 3
Eugene, OR 97401

www.wipfandstock.com

PAPERBACK ISBN: 979-8-3852-0613-1
HARDCOVER ISBN: 979-8-3852-0614-8
EBOOK ISBN: 979-8-3852-0615-5

02/15/24

Scripture quotations marked NIV are taken from the Holy Bible, New International Version® (NIV®), copyright © 1973, 1978, 1984, 2011 by Biblica, Inc.™ Used by permission of Zondervan. All rights reserved worldwide. www.zondervan.com

"In today's deeply divided world, the term 'evangelism' often evokes discomfort among both Christians and non-Christians. Regrettably, this discomfort has led to a significant detachment within much of the twenty-first-century church. This book offers an insightful and bold exploration of what evangelism truly entails, simultaneously rendering the concept more approachable for everyday believers. I applaud David Schaal for his comprehensive grasp of the subject and his pastoral dedication to rekindling the church's engagement with this fundamental aspect of its mission."

—**TANNER PEAKE,** president, Every Home for Christ International

"*Speak Good News* is a divinely pivotal, on-time reminder of the unabated truth that the gospel changes everything. This book affirms that the church *can* in fact fulfill its ecclesiological and missiological potential according to Scripture, and that every disciple has the spiritual DNA to speak good news soundly, boldly, intelligently, relevantly, lovingly, and humbly. David Schaal writes, awakening the heart of the church with fresh fire and passion for everyday gospel witness and challenging us not to allow what has not worked in the past to derail from the kingdom mandate of the present and redemptive promise of the future. Without question, this is the book the church needs to seize one of its finest hours of biblical and practical evangelism. Every disciple can speak the good news of Jesus—everywhere we go."

—**KANITA RUTLEY,** founder and CEO, She Saves a Nation

"David Schaal takes us through his life journey—from childhood with Jehovah's Witnesses to adulthood with the Marine Corps and his own salvation story—how God used these experiences to shape his deep passion and skill in evangelism. This book will encourage you to share your story and bring more people to Jesus. An easy-to-read, humorous, and practical book to inspire you in speaking good news with people each day."
—**ASHLEY TEE,** founder, 3cmSpace

"I've never met anybody who has as much passion as David Schaal to equip the rest of us to speak good news. I've known David since we were young adults, and he has been a constant source of encouragement to me on the subject and urgency of talking to others about Jesus. He's always been in my corner, and by writing this wonderful book, he has placed himself in your corner, too! Thank you, friend, for providing this much-needed gift to the rest of us."
—**KURT JOHNSTON,** pastor of NextGen ministries, Saddleback Church

"As lead pastor of David Schaal's home church, I have the privilege of seeing his passion for evangelism on full display. So, when you are reading the stories of how his life was transformed and learning the heart of Christ for every soul through David's words, I can honestly say this book is more impartational than informational. The authority that David carries on the topic is a result of truly living out the Great Commission, and he rightly and boldly invites us to do the same."
—**BRANDON CORMIER,** lead pastor, Zeal Church

"I have waited for David Schaal to write this book for over thirty years. During that time, David has always set the pace in encouraging and equipping the church to be active in sharing their faith. In *Speak Good News*, David offers the church a fresh perspective on understanding evangelism and easy onramps for any Jesus follower to engage others in spiritual conversations. If you are a pastor, church leader, or faithful Christian who desires to see more people hear about the love of Jesus, this book is written for you."

—**BENNY PEREZ,** lead pastor, ChurchLV

Speak Good News

This book is dedicated to my two favorite "Js"—
My Jesus and My Julie!

I dedicate this book to the glory of Jesus Christ. From the moment I embraced the profound love you bestowed upon me, my desire has been for everyone I encounter to experience the same. This book aims to equip your followers with the necessary tools to joyfully proclaim your praises, much like a bride boasts about her bridegroom. May those devoted to you fall even more deeply in love, a love that propels them to continuously speak your name and share your good news with those who are yet to embrace your grace, redemption, and boundless love.

This book is dedicated to Julie, the love of my life. I am immensely grateful to you and the unwavering love and companionship that has been the bedrock of both my personal and ministerial journey. Throughout our pastoral ministry in local churches, your enduring encouragement and steadfast support have been instrumental in empowering me to embrace and fulfill my calling and passion fully. Your consistent prayer covering has been a source of strength and resilience, providing a firm foundation for all I do. Your exceptional wisdom and insightful counsel make you my most trusted advisor. Your guidance has not only been a compass for navigating the difficulties of ministry but has also enriched my personal growth. You are an invaluable partner in moments of challenge and triumph, shaping my perspective and fortifying my resolve. I am profoundly thankful for the love, home, and family we share together.

They called them back and warned them that they were on no account ever again to speak or teach in the name of Jesus. But Peter and John spoke right back, "Whether it's right in God's eyes to listen to you rather than to God, you decide. **As for us, there's no question—we can't keep quiet about what we've seen and heard."**

—Acts 4:18–20, *The Message*

Contents

Foreword by Kevin G. Harney — ix
Acknowledgments — xiii
Introduction — xv

Chapter 1	What Gave Evangelism a Bad Name?	1
Chapter 2	Redeeming Evangelism	15
Chapter 3	The Anatomy of Mission	28
Chapter 4	The Barrier of Sin	42
Chapter 5	Not Wanting to Be Confrontational	56
Chapter 6	Not Feeling Good (Holy) Enough	66
Chapter 7	Not Knowing What to Say: Part 1	77
Chapter 8	Not Knowing What to Say: Part 2	88
Chapter 9	Tell Your Story!	100
Chapter 10	Ways to Speak Good News!	111

Appendix A: Mission Flowchart — 125
Appendix B: How to Tell Your Story — 127
Bibliography — 133

Foreword

Three of the biggest reasons I read a book are: the author, the topic, and the potential impact on my life. Let me put it another way. I am drawn to books where I can confidently say:

- I trust the writer,
- I need to learn what is being written about, and
- I know I will experience some kind of valuable life transformation.

The book you hold in your hand (or are listening to right now) checks all three of these boxes beautifully!

The Writer: I have known David Schaal for many years and every time we have talked, prayed, shared a meal, or interacted in any way, I have come away more in love with Jesus and more on fire to speak the good news of Jesus to the people I encounter in my life. David's mind is strategic and his heart is tender. This is a powerful combination you will notice all through this book. He is deeply humble and seeks to learn from anyone who is effective in sharing faith in natural and organic ways. Because of this, you will find that when he writes, he draws from a deep reservoir of ancient and modern thinkers that help inform his ideas and teaching. David is a good man and if you ever have a chance to sit and talk with him, you will find that the winsome and gracious spirit that comes through his writing is an accurate reflection of who he is in the real world.

FOREWORD

The Topic: The focus of this book is more than important; it is urgent! We live in a bad news world and human hearts are starving for good news. Followers of Jesus have it. We have testimonies of God's saving and transformational power. We have met the hope of the world. We know the story of Jesus, the Messiah.

The question is, why do so many Jesus-loving Christians avoid evangelism? Why don't we joyfully jump into this call of our Savior? In the pages of this book, David thoughtfully and practically looks at many of the hurdles that get in the way of Jesus followers doing the very thing they want to do . . . speak the good news in ways that friends and family members can understand and receive. When we see the obstacles to evangelism and have a clear strategy to get past them, we will find ourselves engaging in more spiritual conversations.

David does a masterful job of helping ordinary believers discover how they can share the extraordinary message of Jesus. With biblical integrity and real-life examples, his book will give you a pathway to naturally articulating the good news that has transformed your life. This book is not about formulas to memorize. It is about truths to follow and organic ways to speak good news. When you do this, telling your story and the story of Jesus will feel natural to you and those you lovingly share with.

The Impact: Some books give rich historical context and lessons. Others dig deep into core biblical and theological truths. Still other books provide practical life lessons. This book does all three with winsome balance.

The very fact that you are reading *Speak Good News* reveals a profound and important truth. You have people in your life who need to encounter Jesus and hear about the hope that only he can offer. You are seeking to be faithful to the call of the Messiah to join him on his mission of making disciples of all nations.

The impact of this book will be multifaceted. You will think deeply about why evangelism can seem so difficult. You will have a new vision of the amazing call to partner with the Living God in bringing the good news of his Son to the world. You will identify many barriers to sharing your faith and discover that every one of them can be hurdled or removed. Best of all, you will be filled with heaven-sent passion to tell your story and share God's good news with people you love. What could be better than that?

KEVIN G. HARNEY

Acknowledgments

Undertaking a project of this magnitude doesn't happen in isolation. I express deep appreciation for the many individuals who have provided invaluable assistance throughout this journey. Having dedicated over thirty years of my life to vocational ministry, the list of people who have contributed to bringing this book to fruition is extensive. While it is impractical to name everyone, the following individuals deserve special mention.

The completion of this book owes much to Julie Schaal's unwavering support, consistently urging me to write daily. Her belief in this project surpasses mere confidence in my abilities; it was a deep conviction that today's Christian church urgently needs to grasp the beauty of speaking the good news of Jesus Christ. I am grateful for the considerable time she invested in proofreading and editing, contributing to the creation of a book that is clear, easy to read, and easy to put into practice.

I owe a tremendous debt of gratitude to Scott Middlebrook, who has been more than an advisor, colleague, and friend to me. Our collaborative journey spans over two decades, during which we have shared prayers and dreams, working in tandem to ignite the passion for the church of Jesus Christ to be active in proclaiming the gospel. Scott, your invaluable contributions have been pivotal in shaping the narrative of our collective journey. The dynamic exchange of ideas, the challenging discussions that have honed our understanding, and the shared aspirations and dreams have all been captured in the pages of this book. Your remarkable skills in wonder and invention have not only enriched my personal

ACKNOWLEDGMENTS

experience but have also been a driving force behind my ability and have significantly influenced my journey in proclaiming the transformative message of Christ.

It is a privilege to be part of Every Home for Christ International, a ministry that has been a beacon of inspiration and a global force in empowering the church to share the truth and love of Jesus Christ for over three-quarters of a century. As both a scholar and practitioner, collaborating with Every Home has been a source of immense joy. Working alongside dedicated individuals such as Scott Middlebrook, Bri Sweatt, and the entire Every Home USA team has been a rewarding experience, particularly in the development of resources aimed at equipping the church in America for active participation in gospel proclamation.

I extend my gratitude to Marcus Dolphens and Hunter Schaal, whose commitment to the principles outlined in this book is evident by their equipping pastors and churches across the country. Their efforts in facilitating training, engaging with local churches, in having intentional gospel conversations with the lost have brought the teaching of this book to life. Their dedication serves as a living testament to the impact and effectiveness of the strategies outlined in the pages to follow. I am deeply thankful to be associated with such a dynamic team and a ministry that continues to play a pivotal role in advancing the mission of sharing the life-giving message of Jesus Christ.

I also want to acknowledge Reagan, Jacob, Allison, Hunter, Victory, Jackson, Ivory, and Silas. A father could not be prouder of his children and grandchildren as I am of you. The heritage of speaking good news is evident in all your lives. You have put the teaching of this book into practice and are teaching your children to do the same. I am also grateful for your dedicated efforts in spearheading the marketing initiatives for this book. Your tireless commitment has played a pivotal role in ensuring that the message of *Speak Good News* reaches a wide audience, making the book accessible to all.

Introduction

THE IMPACT OF SPEAKING GOOD NEWS

While growing up in the 1970s and early 80s in the Central Coast town of Paso Robles, California, I knew that there was something different about me. Not just myself but my entire family and the close friends of my family. The only real close friends I was allowed to have were those who shared our same religious beliefs. During the first seventeen and a half years of my life, I was raised in a religious organization known as the Jehovah's Witnesses. A core belief of this religion is that one must actively share one's faith as part of one's formation and service to God. The name of the organization declares such. Spending one to two hours each week going home to home sharing the Jehovah's Witnesses faith in my community was a common practice of my childhood.

Being different was not just something I felt about myself; it was something my classmates and peers thought. They knew that the one kid in class who would not salute the flag and say the Pledge of Allegiance (yes, we did this in the 70s) was David. They knew the kid who would not celebrate holidays or attend a birthday party was David. They did not know why; they knew it had something to do with my religion. They also knew that there was a good chance that David and one of his family members, dressed up in a suit and tie, might knock on their door on Saturday morning, interrupting their Saturday morning cartoons. David would visit their neighborhood, trying to sell or give away literature from

INTRODUCTION

his church. Over the twelve years of my primary education, I am sure I knocked on the doors of most of my classmates at least once, if not numerous times.

There was no hostility between my peers and me; we just seemed to have an understanding. They seemed to accept me for who I was, and I did the same with them; we would act and treat each other as classmates at school. Things began to change during my junior and senior years of high school. I was maturing as a young adolescent, and my boldness to think for myself and ability to process thoughts independently began to develop. My classmates began to ask me questions they had wanted to for most of the time that we had known each other. This was when Mike started inviting me to his church's youth group. I always declined, but that did not stop him from asking me. Mike was and is a gifted communicator. He would listen to what I was interested in and try to engage me in conversations that he could put a spiritual twist to. This is evangelism.

Mike was not the only classmate who tried to engage me in conversations about faith. Janet, Christen, Shelia, Cindy, Jay, Winnie, and others tried to share with me. Then there was my friend Tracy. Tracy was not only one of the brightest students in my class, but she was also, in my eyes, one of the prettiest. Tracy knew I had a crush on her, and she used that knowledge to capture my attention whenever she wanted to share her faith with me. I was a willing audience, listening to whatever she had to say. Tracy was intentionally engaging me in spiritual conversations by constantly interjecting a spiritual component into our talk of homework, sports, or weekend activities. This is what I would call "Speaking Good News."

Tracy soon became one of my closest friends during my senior year of high school. I enjoyed hanging out with her, not just because of my schoolboy crush but because there was something authentic and pure about her. I realized this was a family trait as I began getting to know Tracy's family. Her mother, father, two sisters, and brother all had something I did not. They had peace. They had love. They had Jesus! Not only did the Erb family share their faith in Jesus, but they also lived it openly. This is an essential attribute of evangelism. Yet, it was odd to me, as I had been raised in a very religious home but never experienced the peace and contentment I witnessed in the Erb family. I knew I was missing something, which led to me asking more questions and Tracy doing her best to answer. That, too, is evangelism.

Over many months and many conversations, I knew something was missing in my life. After graduation and going our separate ways during the summer, Tracy and I tried our best to keep in touch. During the summer of 1983, I went to the elders of the local Kingdom Hall and informed them that I was beginning to think differently about my faith. My heart was beginning to change due to what I was learning and experiencing from my "born again" Christian friends. By the end of my meeting with the elders, I found myself "disfellowshipped" from the religion. This meant I was to have absolutely no association with any other Jehovah's Witnesses, including my family members. I felt lost and abandoned. I did not know what to do or where to go.

I visited Tracy on the campus of Westmont College, a Christian school in Santa Barbara, California. Tracy and I went for a walk around campus and we ended up in the small chapel. Tracy, fully knowing what I had been through with my family and religion, looked me in the eye and asked, "David, what are you going to do about it?" "Do about what?" I asked. "Your faith!" she replied. "What are you going to do about your faith?" At that moment, I remember thinking, "How can I not say yes to this Jesus?" That day, my life changed, and so did my eternity. It did not happen over one conversation but over hundreds. It did not happen in a moment, but it took over a year. That, my friend, is evangelism. It is a *process* of Christians living out their faith and intentionally engaging others in spiritual conversations that lead to speaking the good news of Jesus Christ.

When I was introduced to Jesus Christ, accepted his forgiveness, and subsequently dedicated my life to serving him, I remember being unable to contain this new truth. I could not be silent. I had to tell as many people as I could. Sadly, I was taken aback by

INTRODUCTION

seeing that few of my fellow Christians carried the same burden of being actively involved in sharing their faith through verbal proclamation. Admittedly, I was a new and somewhat naïve follower of Jesus Christ. I remember asking more seasoned Christians about opportunities to go and tell others about Jesus like I did when I was a Jehovah's Witness. Often, I would be told that Christians do not purposefully go out and share as I did as a Jehovah's Witness; we invite people to church or take advantage of a situation that may present itself.

The idea of intentionally engaging non-Christians with the purpose of evangelizing them was left to those who had shown a gift in this area. The common misconception was that sharing one's faith was not for all Christians but for that small group of people with reputations or giftedness as evangelists. I did not have any peace with the above-mentioned misconception, leading me to serve as an evangelism trainer, my first ministry position in church. We used and practiced the teachings of the *Evangelism Explosion* curriculum[1] and *Becoming a Contagious Christian*.[2] Both proved to be excellent tools for training the Christian church to share its faith.

Over the last thirty-two years, I have served Christ's church in various pastoral and leadership roles. Through these years, my passion for evangelism has never wavered. In the spring of 2014, I took a course at Fuller Theological Seminary entitled Focused Lives. This course was based on a text by that same name, authored by J. Robert Clinton. In it Clinton says:

> A focused life is a life dedicated to exclusively carrying out God's unique purposes through it, by identifying the focal issues, that is, the major role, life purpose, unique methodology, or ultimate contributions, which allows an increasing prioritization of life's activities around the focal issues and results in a satisfying life of being and doing.[3]

1. Kennedy, *Evangelism Explosion*.
2. Hybels et al., *Becoming a Contagious Christian*.
3. Clinton, *Focused Lives*, 53.

INTRODUCTION

This course was both life-changing and purpose-confirming for me. My calling is to help equip Christ's followers to participate in sharing their love for and faith in Jesus Christ to a lost and dying world. After completing this course, I realized I needed to prioritize my life's activities and live out my calling. The way I pastored and preached began to change. The way I lived my life in my community and the way I led my family all changed. Since then, I have been on a mission to finish well by living out my calling daily.

In the pages to come, I would like to explore some of the ideas and practices of what we call evangelism. I hope to answer some of the questions and clear away many of the misconceptions associated with this beautiful practice. I assume that most Christians understand evangelism to mean the sharing of one's faith in Jesus Christ with others, hoping they, too, would decide to put their faith in and follow Jesus. At the same time, these same Christians find it difficult to participate in engaging non-Christians in spiritual conversations. This book is primarily written for this audience. I share the results of two national studies that looked at the practices and perceptions of evangelism in the lives of the everyday Christ-follower. The data shared informed me that there are some gaps that need to be filled. I conclude this book by sharing ways to overcome the barriers Christ's followers allow in their lives that prevent them from speaking good news to the lost. I end the book by sharing some fresh perspectives on engaging others in spiritual conversations.

1

What Gave Evangelism a Bad Name?

Have you ever played the game of telephone? Maybe you have heard it called "whispers" or something similar. The game of telephone was created to be an educational game, training children in their listening skills. This is a game, usually played by three or more children, where the first child whispers a word or phrase in the ear of the next child, and then that child shares it with the next. After the last child hears the word or phrase whispered in their ear, they say it aloud for the whole group to hear. Most of the time, what was communicated by the first child is vastly different from what is recited at the end. There are many reasons for this. Maybe one of the children did not hear properly and then shared what they thought they heard. Or perhaps a child did not pronounce the phrase correctly, and that caused the next child to try and figure out what was said.

    I remember playing this game in elementary school, mostly on rainy days when we had to stay in for recess. We would play with twenty to thirty students. I do have to admit that, to make things a little interesting, my friends and I would deliberately change the word or phrase to see if we could get a big laugh. We would make slight variations, changing a word such as *blue* to *green*. Or, if the word was *fountain*, we might change it to a rhyming word like *mountain*. However, our teachers were always on to us. To find out who changed the word or phrase from the original, they would start at the beginning and ask each child what they heard and what they said. Inevitably, they would find the person (me or one of my friends) who made the change.

If there is one word that evokes feelings of discomfort when spoken to Christians and non-Christians alike, it is the word *evangelism*. For the Christ-follower, this word brings feelings of guilt, shame, and inadequacy, for they know that, on some level, they should be participating in evangelistic activities, but they are not. Non-Christ-followers see this word as akin to high-pressure salespersons and overbearing proselytizing from the street-corner preacher. And we certainly don't want to be viewed in such a way, right? As a result, evangelism has been relegated to the function of the select gifted people in the church, or the definition has been diluted to include all church activities.

Now, I understand that asking questions such as "What gave evangelism a bad name?" can open a can of worms. There may be just as many opinions as there are individuals you ask. Some may state:

- The judgmental reputation of the church.
- Having to tell people how bad they are.
- Condemning attitudes and superiority of proclaimers.
- Canned methodologies and programs.
- It seems more like church recruitment.
- The political reputation of the church.
- Pushing people to make a decision.
- Pressure to "close the deal."

I do not doubt that an entire book could be written on this subject alone.

How about you?

> What do you think is the reason, or reasons, that evangelism has a less-than-favorable reputation?

WHAT GAVE EVANGELISM A BAD NAME?

To determine what gave the word *evangelism* a bad name, it would be helpful to look back at the original idea of evangelism and then trace the history to see what went wrong. In chapter 2, I will outline and define the meaning behind the word *evangelism* and encourage Christ-followers to participate in this beautiful practice. In this chapter, I aim at only highlighting one idea as to what gave evangelism a bad name.

As a disclaimer, there may be many reasons why evangelism does not receive the high praise as one may think it should. The following is only meant to guide us to figure out one reason evangelism is not as popular as it should be.

To begin, consider these words of Marshall Shelley:

> Want a good 46-word overview of church history? Here's one from former U.S. Senate chaplain Richard Halverson: "The church began in Jerusalem as a fellowship of men and women centered on Jesus Christ. It went to Greece and became a philosophy. It went to Rome and became an institution. It went to Europe and became a culture. It came to America and became an enterprise."[1]

In my mind's eye, I can see individuals from Jerusalem, Greece, Rome, Europe, and America standing in line, whispering to each other what they think Christianity is and how to share it with others. What started in Jerusalem differs from what we may hear today in America.

So, starting from the beginning, let us conduct a brief survey on the movement of Christianity through the centuries and regions of the world. By no means is the following to be an exhaustive examination of the history of the Christian church. This cursory guide will help us examine why evangelism is not popular. While we look at these five time stamps in the church's history, it is essential to understand that we are only examining the one aspect of God's mission that we call "evangelism."

---

1. Shelley, "Heart & Soul."

SPEAK GOOD NEWS

JERUSALEM

Looking at the New Testament writings, we understand how the Christian church started and how it began to expand. The book of Acts gives us this historical picture, starting shortly after Jesus' ascension and the arrival of the Holy Spirit. In Acts 2, we see the beginning of the evangelization of the surrounding people. The scene is the feast of Pentecost. This annual harvest festival occurs seven weeks after Passover, where the Israelites would bring the first fruits of their harvest as a sacrificial offering. We read that there were God-fearing Jews from every nation under heaven staying in Jerusalem (Acts 2:5). People from no less than sixteen regions are mentioned in verses 8–11. The crowds were perplexed because these were Galileans speaking in different languages, languages that only people from those represented areas of the world would understand.

What were these Galileans sharing? In verse 11, we read that they shared the "wonders" of God. The Greek word used here is *megaleíos*, which can be expressed as "great, glorious, wonderful works," "the outworking of the greatness of God's power and glory." These 120 God-fearing believers shared his wonders with people who had not heard the truth about Jesus. This is evangelism.

These events sparked the people's interest to know more, so Peter began to share with them. He gives them a historical understanding of what had happened concerning Jesus Christ, why he came, what he did, and where he is now. Peter outlines Jesus' life, death, and resurrection within his teaching, identifying him as the Messiah. Many of those hearing Peter were convicted and asked him, "Brothers, what must we do?" (2:37). Peter told them to turn from what they trusted in and toward Jesus, looking to him to forgive them of their sins and then be baptized and receive the gift of the Holy Spirit as a deposit of God's seal on them. We read that Peter continued to share and answer questions that led to three thousand or more putting their faith in Jesus that day.

It would be easy to look at Peter and think, "Wow, he must have been a very inspirational speaker, influencing three thousand people to put their faith in Jesus." While that may be true, let us not forget about the other 120 believers who publicly shared the wonders of God with others. This is evangelism! Their sharing of the things of God sparked interest in those they were sharing with, which led them to want to hear more. As Paul reminded the church in Corinth, "I planted the seed, Apollos watered it, but God has been making it grow" (1 Cor 3:6). The church began to grow that day. We then read that those who had now put their faith in Jesus began to live differently. They listened to the apostles teach, and they ate and prayed together. They shared their possessions with anyone who needed them, enjoying fellowship and praising God. God continued to add to the number of people putting their faith in Jesus (Acts 2:40–47).

Reading how the 120 believers started to declare the wonders of God to strangers in a large city causes me to ask, "Why? Were they told to do so?" I might also wonder, "Were they given a script or a model to follow?" I believe the answer to both of these questions is no.

There may be another angle to consider. Were they trying to obey Jesus' commission to the church to go out and make disciples? Other questions may arise, such as: Did Jesus change their life so much that they could not keep the message of salvation and forgiveness to themselves? Was it the presence of the Holy Spirit working in their lives? The answers to all of these questions are an unequivocal are yes, yes, and yes!

In the very beginning, the Christian church began as a fellowship of men and women centered on Jesus Christ. They were declaring his greatness. They were telling as many as they could. They intentionally engaged others in spiritual conversations that led to the people across the Roman Empire hearing the gospel. Being centered on and in Jesus Christ should naturally provoke us to share his wonders with all who will listen.

SPEAK GOOD NEWS
GREECE

On the day of Pentecost, God-fearing Jews from every nation under heaven heard Christ's followers share the praises of God, and they heard Peter share the gospel in its entirety. Over the next few decades, Christianity grew as these new believers returned home and shared their new understanding of God and faith with many. They, again, were evangelizing! They were sharing with others this newfound truth. We also see the Christian church comprising more than just Jewish converts. We now read of gentiles coming to faith and Paul being set apart as an apostle to the gentiles, laying the foundations of the gospel across the Roman Empire. Of importance to note is that during his second missionary journey, we read that Paul finds himself in Athens, Greece.

Paul is there to spread the truth of Jesus Christ to all who would listen. He is preaching in the synagogues, and his reputation begins to spread. Athens is a very philosophical city that boasts of being the architect of Western civilization and democracy. We find in Acts 17 that a group of philosophers begins to debate Paul, claiming he is advocating for some foreign god since he is preaching about the resurrection of Jesus Christ. Some think he is a lunatic. He is invited to the Areopagus to continue his talk with other Greek philosophers. These philosophers spent all day sharing and hearing new ideas and thoughts. So, Paul takes advantage of the audience before him and begins contextualizing the gospel. He sees a tomb inscribed with the phrase, "To an unknown god." Paul then explains who this God is that they are worshiping. Here, Paul teaches us a critical aspect of evangelizing.

> People *are* interested in spiritual matters. We need to find areas of common ground and build upon them, and draw a connection to Jesus.

After Paul shares with the group of philosophers, most disagree and even sneer at him, for they cannot come to terms with the resurrection. However, some do believe, and they leave and follow Paul on his journey.

Now to this point, we have talked about and used the word *evangelism* to speak of the practice of sharing the good news of Jesus Christ. I will dive deeper into the meaning of evangelism in the next chapter. However, let's take a brief look at this word, *evangel-ism*. In layman's terms, the word *evangel* translates from the prefix *ev-*, meaning good, and *angel*, meaning message or messenger. If we add the suffix *-ism*, the term then describes a distinctive practice, system, philosophy, or ideology. For example, the *Oxford English Dictionary* gives the following definition for these words. *Consumerism* is "a cultural model that promotes the acquisition of goods, and especially the purchase of goods, as a vehicle for personal satisfaction and economic stimulation." *Atheism* is "the disbelief or lack of belief in the existence of God or Gods."[2]

One can argue that after the gospel was brought to the philosophers of Greece, the Christian message became diluted by some, becoming much more of an ideology. Even taking the word *evangel-ism*, perhaps denotes it more as a philosophy or practice of a certain ideology. Regardless, the word *evangelism* is seen as akin to proselytizing, the action of attempting to convert someone from one religion, belief, or opinion to another. This may seem insignificant, yet when we recognize that the church was first seen as a fellowship of men and women centered on Jesus Christ, then becoming more of a philosophy or ideology, we should not be surprised that it would again morph into something distinct from what was first vocalized.

ROME

Christianity was now growing into the entire known world. While Paul and others had brought the teaching of Jesus Christ to many regions, none were more important than Rome. This city was the epicenter of all civilization. The Roman Empire had the most

2. Soanes and Stevenson, *Concise Oxford English Dictionary*.

SPEAK GOOD NEWS

powerful military force on earth. The phrase "All roads lead to Rome" was a true statement. Roads were built to aid not only the military but to increase commerce as well. Even more, Christianity is becoming more accepted as the years moved on. In 312 AD, the emperor of Rome, Constantine, converted to Christianity. The following year, Constantine and Licinius issued the Edict of Milan, making Christianity a legal religion of Rome. Philosophical Christianity took its place in Rome, as two leaders, Athanasius and Arius, began to dispute the deity of Jesus Christ.

Arius (Arianism) did not believe in the full deity of Jesus Christ. On the other hand, Athanasius believed that Jesus is both fully man and fully God. Now, Emperor Constantine did not like this division in the church. He told the bishops that "It is worse than war" because it had eternal ramifications for the soul. He asked for a meeting of the eighteen hundred bishops to come and settle things. Three hundred gathered and ultimately adopted an early version of the Nicene Creed.

With the Edict of Milan and the Nicene Creed, we can see the Christian church becoming an institution. This is the beginning of Christendom, laying the foundation for the Christian church to be the majority, carrying power and control. We also see, arguably, the institution of the Roman Catholic Church come to be, even though Catholics would trace their beginnings to Jesus Christ and their first pope, St. Peter. The institution now saw itself meeting in church buildings with people attending and obtaining membership. This establishment grew until there was a separation in 1517, due to Martin Luther's penning of his Ninety-Five Theses. Luther specifically stood against some of the teachings and practices of the institutionalized church. Just six years later, Ulrich Zwingli, a priest in Switzerland, brought the German-led Reformation to other parts of Europe.[3] Many who protested with them became the Protest-ants. In the Western world, we now had two similar, but different, Christian institutions, Roman Catholicism and Protestantism. Both confessed Christ, but both had distinct perspectives. It was not long before the Protestants saw a split in their

---

3. Curtis et al., *100 Most Important Events*, 98.

institutionalized faith. A young leader named Jacob Arminius challenged John Calvin's teaching on grace being only for the elect and his view on predestination. This then produced those who favored Calvinism and those who favored Arminianism.

This cursory account of church history is to get to the point of seeing its effect on evangelism.

> No longer is the Christian church looked upon as a family of believers proclaiming the goodness of God. It is now a philosophy housed in different institutions.

No longer is evangelization seen as sharing the truth and love of Jesus Christ with the goal of making disciples, but its central focus moves to sharing the teachings of a particular institution or -ism. We no longer invite people to know Jesus but to join our local institution (church). In commenting on this detour from the Great Commission's call to ". . . go and make disciples of all nations . . . teaching them to obey everything I have commanded you" (Matt 28:19). Dallas Willard writes, "But in place of Christ's plan, historical drift has substituted 'Make converts (to a particular "faith and practice") and baptize them into church membership.'"[4] I would add: "and teach them to understand and obey the constitution and bylaws of the local church." The "whisper" of the practice of evangelism can now be seen through a brief lens into church history. Things have greatly changed from what we read in the New Testament.

EUROPE

The institutionalized Christian church, both Roman Catholic and Protestant,[5] began to grow throughout Europe for many centuries. From Constantine's and Licinius's issue of the Edict of Milan, Christianity was not only free from the majority of persecution it

---

4. Willard, *Great Omission*, 5
5. Here I am assessing the Western church.

once suffered; it was now experiencing popularity and power. The church began to grow because people wanted to belong to a respectable religion with official sponsorship.[6] This growth had more to do with political sovereignty than evangelizing people that did not know Jesus Christ and the greatness of God's power and glory.

The church's movement from institution to culture was happening simultaneously as more and more nations began to identify as Christian nations. Two historical events can be seen as a catalyst to the birth of cultural Christianity. In 1521, England's king, Henry VIII, wanted to divorce his wife, as she could not bear him a child. Furthermore, he desired to marry the younger and more attractive Anne Boleyn. To do so, he would need approval from the pope. To Henry's dismay, the pope refused the request. This angered the king, and he subsequently appointed Thomas Cranmer as archbishop of Canterbury, officially forming the Church of England. Archbishop Cranmer granted the divorce, and King Henry and Anne were quickly married, producing Charles, their son, as an heir.[7]

Not long after, the English Parliament passed the Acts of Supremacy, which made the king (or anyone who sat on the throne) the highest and supreme head of the Church of England. This is an office the monarchy still holds today. Whether on purpose or not, this then established England as a Christian nation, giving rise to all rules and instructions for the citizens of England to follow. To say you were *English* was synonymous with saying you were *Christian*. In 1662, the Act of Uniformity emboldened this cultural Christianity. This meant strict adherence to the liturgy described in the *Book of Common Prayer*. Furthermore, one had to follow the Act of Uniformity to hold public office in government or the church[8].

You may ask, "What does this have to do with evangelism?" If you are Christian by citizenship or birth, then there is no need or urgency to share your faith with others. For example, my first

---

6. Curtis et al., 100 *Most Important Events*, 33.
7. Curtis et al., 100 *Most Important Events*, 102.
8. González, *Story of Christianity*, 73.

experience with understanding cultural Christianity came in 1984, shortly after I put my faith in Jesus Christ. Like most new believers, I wanted to tell as many people as possible. After leaving my Jehovah's Witnesses family, I lived with my birth mother in Southern California for a few months. I remember talking with her at the kitchen table, a proud Canadian raised in the province of Newfoundland. I asked my mother if she was a Christian and if she was "saved." She staunchly looked me in the eye and said, "I was baptized as an infant in the Church of England, my father was a deacon in the church, and I attended Sunday school when I was a little girl. *Yes*, I am a Christian!"

Cultural Christianity, spiritual rules and regulations handed down by governmental leaders, and so on, were not accepted by all. During this same time in church history, a growing group of Christians wanted to go back and live by what they read in the Bible, devoid of all the added instructions from the government. These people wanted a pure and biblical Christianity, thus they became known as "Puritans." These Puritans wanted to go further than just reforming the church. They wanted their lives to be ruled by the Holy Spirit and to receive their instruction from the Scriptures, and instead of being controlled by a powerful institution, they desired to be known as a family made up of brothers and sisters where God was working in their hearts. In 1620, these Puritans, also known as "Separatists" (those wanting to be separated from the Church of England, or Anglican Church), decided that the only place to see such a church was to take it to the New World (America)[9].

AMERICA

These Puritans, also called "Pilgrims," landed in the New World to establish this untainted expression of the kingdom of God. Like many well-meaning endeavors, what started with the purist of intentions, over time, became something different. As more

---

9. Curtis et al., *100 Most Important Events*, 116.

SPEAK GOOD NEWS

and more people migrated to the New World, they also brought their well-meaning desires and interests, which eventually created American culture.

America is widely known for its economic system of capitalism and free-market enterprise. Free-market enterprise refers to having minimal barriers regarding the exchange of wealth or the transaction of goods and services. Every aspect of the American landscape has a direct connection to capitalism and free enterprise. Our free-market system has influenced our education, hospitals, media, government, and even institutions of religion.

While churches are set up as nonprofit organizations, there is still the need to generate revenue to pay the operational expenses. When I was pastoring, I was known as, if anything, a pastor with an affinity for evangelism and reaching the lost. However, even so, I knew we had to do other things to "market" the church to non-attendees. We ran a weekly ad in the local newspaper inviting all to our services. We also ran ads on the local radio station advertising our new sermon series or special services. We sponsored the Chicago Cubs baseball games on our local radio station during the season, airing a church invitational spot during the game. We were members of the city's chamber of commerce to show the businesses we were invested in the community. I have heard of some churches using other marketing strategies, like offering door prizes to first-time guests on Easter Sunday or renting a helicopter to drop Easter eggs down to the children below.

I am not condemning these activities at all. As I mentioned, as a pastor, I always looked for opportunities to get new people to come and visit our church. More visitors meant the possibility of the church growing. The more the church grew, the more likely our income would grow, which meant we had more money to invest in kingdom growth. However, the effect such practices have had on evangelism has not always been positive. This is one of the points that John Drane makes in his book *The McDonaldization of the Church*. Working from the theme of sociologist George Ritzer,[10] Drane looks at how many churches function with the

---

10. Ritzer, *McDonaldization of Society*.

same business model as the fast-food chain McDonald's, where everything is packaged and delivered to you in a timely manner. Our worship, the liturgy or message, and even the giving of tithes and offerings are done precisely to make it easy for the consumer. Drane comments, "A theology that comes pre-packaged, and in which there are no loose ends, is not true to life, nor can it adequately reflect the richness of the gospel."[11] All of this is to say that many times evangelism is reduced to just inviting people to a perfectly planned service. At the same time, I agree that when we invite people to our local church service, we practice evangelism. However, this is sometimes the extent of evangelism activities for many faithful Christians.

To further the argument that a business or enterprise approach has given evangelism a less-than-favorable name, we only need to look at some of the methodologies we are encouraged to follow. There is nothing wrong with using a method, formula, or program to engage others in spiritual conversations. However, where I would caution would be in the expectation of instant results of such programs and methods. Many of these methodologies lead the proclaimer to try and "close the deal," if you will. This is a sales mentality, when a salesman tries to convince someone to purchase a certain item, such as a car. Many of Christ's followers believe they need to close the deal by having someone say yes to Jesus or have them say a "sinner's prayer." When this does not happen, feelings of doubt and insecurity arise, discouraging the Christ-follower from participating in evangelism activities.

So far, we have talked about the advancement of the Christian church through a very narrow lens of church history, only to draw some conclusions to answer the question of what gave evangelism a bad name. This is not an indictment on the Christian church but more of an explanation to try and move us to a better understanding of the practice of evangelism. Wherever we see the church moving, we eventually see it being influenced by the culture it is living in. It is no surprise to see the American church taking on

---

11. Drane, *McDonaldization of the Church*, 43.

some of the more visible attributes of the capitalist, free-market American culture.

    This chapter is meant to be a cursory look at the history of the church through the ages to show how the contextual cultural influences of philosophy, institutions, culture, and business may have affected how Christians through the ages have seen the practice of evangelism. Like the game of telephone, what was spoken and purposed initially for healthy evangelism and discipleship has turned into something quite different. From the philosophies of Athens to the institutionalized settings of Rome and Western Europe, and then on to the setting up of state churches in such nations as England and the free-market enterprises of America, the church becomes enmeshed with its cultural environment. This has particularly affected the church's engagement in healthy mission, evangelism, and discipleship. In the next chapter, we will take up the same approach as my elementary teacher and return to the beginning. We will look at the initial understanding of the idea of the call of the church to communicate the truth and love of Jesus Christ, with the hope of redeeming evangelism.

2

Redeeming Evangelism

I have fond memories of growing up in a small community on the Central Coast of California, where I first experienced the blessings of redemption. I remember walking the streets of my hometown, collecting soda pop bottles that people had discarded. The phrase "return for redemption" or "return for deposit" was written on each bottle. I knew if I collected enough empty bottles, I could take them to the local grocery store and redeem them for cash. Well, at least I would get ten cents for the regular sixteen-ounce bottles, and if I was fortunate enough to find the larger half-liter bottles, those paid twenty-five cents. If I collected enough bottles each day, I would have enough money to purchase my own soda pop or favorite candy bar. The bottles would then become *redeemed* so they could be returned to service for their original purpose. It was in that same small Central Coast town that, years later, I would fully understand what it truly means to be redeemed.

The *Merriam-Webster Dictionary* defines the word *redeem* as a transitive verb meaning "to buy back" or, better yet, "to get or win back." Biblically, redemption would also have the connotation of being set free—freeing from the chains of slavery or prison.[1] Redemption is the bedrock of the good news we read of in the

---

1. Elwell and Comfort, *Tyndale Bible Dictionary*, 1114.

SPEAK GOOD NEWS

Bible. In Genesis, we read of God's original plan for humankind, to have a living, tangible relationship where each enjoys the company of the other. We also read in Genesis chapter 3 that this plan was attacked due to the original sin of Adam and Eve, who disobeyed God by eating from the forbidden tree. From the point of the fall of man, and starting in verse 15 of Genesis 3, we read the story of God's love for his creation, that he sets in place a plan to *redeem* what the enemy has stolen. Jesus Christ becomes our Redeemer by giving his life in place for us all. Paul said that we were bought with a price (1 Cor 6:20). In essence, Jesus redeemed us by giving his life for ours so that we can experience God's original plan for his creation, to have a living, tangible, loving relationship with God our Father.

Those of us who have been redeemed and have put our faith and trust in Jesus Christ alone for our salvation should naturally be unable to contain our joy. It should move us to tell others how they, too, can experience redemption back to the original purpose of enjoying a living, loving, tangible relationship with God our Father. The psalmist said this: "Give thanks to the LORD, for he is good; his love endures forever. Let the redeemed of the LORD tell their story, those he redeemed from the hand of the foe . . ." (Ps 107:1–2). I like how David connects the need to acknowledge what God has done for us as good with something that needs to be communicated.

> In short, redeemed people redeem people by telling their stories and introducing others to the Redeemer.

This is evangelism!

Evangelism is one of those words, actions, and phenomena that needs to be redeemed in Christ-followers' lives today, to be loosened and free from the prison it currently seems to be in. There is a need for evangelism to be set free from the negative narrative that many see it. Pastors tell me that when they try to have an evangelism training course, very few, if anybody, show up. In 2018, the Barna Group asked 1,004 U.S. churchgoers what spiritual activity most spurred their excitement. They provided a list to choose from: worship, serving those in need, building community, preaching/teaching, discipleship, and evangelism. Only 7 percent of churchgoers were excited about or interested in church training and/or providing opportunities in evangelism. At the same time, 50 percent were interested in serving those in need.[2] The Barna Group conducted similar research in 2020 on behalf of Every Home for Christ. In this study, participants were asked if they had ever attended a class or had been given instructions on sharing their faith. Only 13 percent indicated they had participated in evangelism training more than twice. 87 percent reported less than twice, with 62 percent saying they had never attended a class or had instruction on how to share their faith.[3] This does not mean our pastors and churches are not providing such classes or opportunities. It does suggest that when pastors and churches offer such training, up to 87 percent of the church does not attend.

It seems as if the church today has gone a long way from what we read in both the Old and New Testaments when it comes to the people of God telling others about his truth and love. When Jeremiah considered not speaking for the Lord, he realized he could not hold the message inside without exploding: "But if I say, "I will not mention his word or speak anymore in his name," his word is in my heart like a fire, a fire shut up in my bones. I am weary of holding it in; indeed, I cannot" (Jer 20:9). When the religious leaders asked Peter and John, two of Jesus' disciples, to stop speaking about Jesus, they replied, "As for us, we cannot help speaking about what we have seen and heard" (Acts 4:20). Their hearts were filled with awe for Jesus and his work for them; thus, there was no way they could be silent. This book aims to help Christ-followers understand the true meaning of evangelism and propose a plan for how we can all participate in redeeming the beautiful act of verbally sharing with others about this wonderful gift we have embraced called the gospel of Jesus Christ.

---

2. Barna, *Translating the Great Commission*, 56.
3. Every Home for Christ, *Reviving Mission*, 49.

SPEAK GOOD NEWS

PROCLAMATION VS. DEMONSTRATION

Over the last few decades, Christians in the United States have become involved in social action aimed at helping people enjoy a better way of life. Christians have led the way in creating hospital systems in nations without healthcare. The same is true with providing education as Christians open schools and take care of orphans and widows.[4] Feeding the hungry, clothing the naked, leading the way in creation care, and participating in social justice are just some ways that the Christian church has stepped up and demonstrated love for one another by living their lives in light of the gospel.

The words Christians share about the love of Jesus must be consistent with how they live their life as a testimony and validation of the gospel they share. The danger comes, though, when the church overly shares the quote (wrongly credited to Francis of Assisi), "Preach the gospel at all times, and when necessary, use words."[5] While this is a beautiful reminder that deeds are just as important as words, quotes and clichés like this can misinform the church that those who demonstrate the gospel with deeds are more important than and superior to those who may proclaim the gospel through words.[6] This has led to the church of Jesus Christ doing many good things for others, but many times stopping short of verbalizing the reason for their service: the love of Jesus, and Jesus' love for them. Critiquing this misquote, Missiologist Ed Stetzer concludes, "The gospel is the declaration of something that actually happened. And since the gospel is the saving work of Jesus, it isn't something we can do, but it is something we must announce. We do live out its implications, but if we are to make the gospel known, we will do so through words."[7] Here, Stetzer supports the need for evangelism to always have a verbal expression. In a meeting with church leaders, Stetzer made this comparison

---

4. Flynn, "Catholic Hospitals."
5. Stanton, "Misquoting Francis of Assisi."
6. Stanton, "Misquoting Francis of Assisi."
7. Stetzer, "Preach the Gospel."

that brings the point home: "Saying, 'Preach the gospel at all times, and when necessary use words,' is like saying, 'Feed the hungry at all times, and when necessary use food'!" Without minimizing the importance of demonstrating the gospel through our good deeds, evangelism, in its purest meaning, will always have a verbal expression. There is no documentation directly attributing this quote to St. Francis of Assisi. It seems chapter 12 of the Rule of 1221, on how the Franciscans should practice their preaching, has been taken out of its original context: "No brother should preach contrary to the form and regulations of the holy church nor unless his minister has permitted his . . . All the Friars . . . should preach by their deeds."[8]

> Duane Liftin declares, "Evangelism is not everything; it is one specific thing. It is the act of giving verbal witness to the gospel, the good news of Jesus Christ."[9]

Evangelism involves using words, but one's deeds empower those words, lived out in the light of the gospel. But often, the American church emphasizes demonstrating the gospel and good deeds more than proclamation. Kingdom work is both proclamation and demonstration. Today, evangelical Christians bring healing to a hurting world by supporting many humanitarian aid organizations. However, they can still fail to proclaim the gospel verbally. Missiologist David Bosch agrees: "Evangelism is the core, heart, or center of mission: it consists in the proclamation of salvation in Christ to nonbelievers, in announcing the forgiveness of sins, in calling people to repentance and faith in Christ, in inviting them to become living members of Christ's earthly community and to begin a life in the power of the Holy Spirit."[10] While Christians should live their lives in light of the gospel with their good works and deeds, they should, at the same time, be willing to proclaim the gospel with their words.

8. Stanton, "Misquoting Francis of Assisi."
9. Litfin, *Word versus Deed*, 47.
10. Bosch, *Transforming Mission*, 11.

SPEAK GOOD NEWS

Serving those in need is vitally important. As one offers the thirsty a cup of water to drink or a meal to the hungry, he or she should, at the same time, offer them the "living water" and/or the "bread of life." This would be demonstration and proclamation working hand in hand. In short, to evangelize, or to participate in evangelism, means to proclaim the good news. What good news? It is the news of what God has done through Christ Jesus for the redemption of humanity.[11] According to the apostle Paul, it is that Christ, according to the Scriptures, died for humanity's sins, was buried, and was raised on the third day (1 Cor 15:3–4). The good news is the gospel of Jesus Christ.

EVANGELISM EXPLAINED BY OTHERS

David Bosch says that evangelism has a "plethora of definitions."[12] Some would argue that evangelism's definition encompasses more than the proclamation of the gospel. In 1918, the Church of England held its Third Committee of Inquiry, in which Archbishop William Temple defined evangelism as "presenting Jesus Christ in the power of the Holy Spirit, that men shall come to put their trust in God through him, to accept him as their Savior, and serve him as their King in the fellowship of his Church."[13] British theologian, Christian apologist, and author Michael Green states that this definition of evangelism includes no less than seven aspects: 1) evangelism is not the same as mission, but one distinct aspect of mission; 2) evangelism is good news about Jesus; 3) evangelism is centered in God the Father; 4) evangelism depends entirely on the Holy Spirit; 5) evangelism means incorporation into the local church; 6) evangelism challenges decisions; and 7) evangelism leads to discipleship.[14] In my experience, definitions like this can add to the confusion surrounding the church's understanding of evangelism. Temple's definition of evangelism may be more of the

---

11. Dubose, *God Who Sends*, 115.
12. Bosch, *Transforming Mission*, 418.
13. Church of England, *Evangelistic Work of the Church*.
14. Green, *Evangelism*, 8–11.

purpose of evangelism. In my opinion, this is a definition of the Great Commission, in which evangelism plays a vital role, as mentioned in point 2, "evangelism is good news about Jesus." William Abraham supports the idea that the definition of evangelism includes a process of "intentional activities which is governed by the goal of initiating people in the kingdom of God for the first time."[15] This definition adds the concept of results to evangelism. Evangelism is an initial invitation into the kingdom of God; what needs more understanding is Abraham's inclusion of primary instruction, prayer, and ensuring that those who respond are brought to baptism or confirmation through the aforementioned proclamation in his explanation of evangelism.

Scott Jones supports Abraham's definition by saying that evangelism is "that set of loving, intentional activities governed by the goal of initiating persons into Christian discipleship in response to the reign of God."[16] Jones argues that evangelism is both proclamation and action. To support this argument, he contrasts someone doing good deeds to gain personal attention with someone doing good deeds to show the unsaved that Christians possess a giving, serving heart. While I would not dispute that Christians need to give and serve others in the name of Christ, serving others in and of itself may not be considered evangelism if it does not have a verbal component.

While the emphasis of my definition is on verbal proclamation, it cannot be separated from being lived out in the life of the proclaimer; evangelism is giving a verbal witness to all that a person has experienced and has grown to understand of Jesus' invitation for all people to be redeemed back into the original relationship for which they were created. Bosch agrees with Abraham and Jones that evangelism consists of more than just proclamation. Bosch is quoted as saying, "This does not suggest that evangelism consists in verbal witness only. It consists in word and deed, proclamation and presence, explanation and example."[17] In saying that

15. Abraham, *Logic of Evangelism*, 95.
16. Jones, *Evangelistic Love*, 29.
17. Bosch, *Transforming Mission*, 430.

evangelism is not only verbal proclamation, Bosch argues that it most certainly does have an inescapable verbal dimension: "The deed without the word is dumb; the word without deed is empty."[18] And that is the point I am making.

Words are empowered by the demonstration of those words. Professor Francis DuBose states that "evangelism is not in the strictest sense 'doing,' that is, apart from 'telling.' Therefore, New Testament evangelism is in the finest sense a process of communication."[19] In a pluralist society, Christians need to proclaim the name of Jesus to give witness to their demonstration.[20]

EVANGELISM DEFINED

Sri Lankan pastor and theologian D. T. Niles is credited with defining evangelism as "One beggar telling another beggar where to get bread."[21] Think about that; the love that one human has for another, that they would share with others who are in the same situation where to find daily food to survive, is a beautiful picture of humanity. Every forgiven person serving Jesus Christ is indebted to the person, group, or church that shared with him or her the good news of how to be free from the penalty of sin. That's why I am still in contact with and love my high school friends Mike and Tracy! It should be a natural outflow of all Christ-followers to be active in telling non-Christ-followers how to find hope, love, and forgiveness through a new life in Jesus Christ. This simple and beautiful act of sharing the good news of what God has done for all people would seem easy for Christ-followers today. This is evangelism!

David Barrett shared over seventy-nine definitions in his text *Evangelize!: A Historical Survey of the Concept*.[22] I will now add my definition to the growing list—not to add to the confusion, but

---

18. Bosch, *Transforming Mission*, 430.
19. Dubose, *God Who Sends*, 117.
20. Newbigin, *Gospel in a Pluralist Society*.
21. Niles, *That They May Have Life*, 96.
22. Barrett, *Evangelize!*, 42–45.

to hopefully bring the understanding into a more precise focus. I present that:

> "Evangelism is intentionally engaging others in spiritual conversations that can lead to sharing the gospel of Jesus Christ."[23]

The English words *evangelism* and *evangelization* come from the Greek (εὐαγγέλιον, ου, τό) *euangelion*. The *Greek-English Lexicon* defines *euangelion* as a reward for good news, or simply as good news.[24] Sam Chan agrees by defining *euangelion* as "to bring good news."[25] Francis DuBose suggests the word *evangelism* is better rendered as "good news-ism," even though one cannot find the noun version of *evangelism* in the New Testament. Instead, it is only found in the verb or action word tense, with the meaning of "proclaim the good news," which naturally connects it to the family of "communication."[26] According to David Barrett, the word *evangelism* is derived from the two words *eu* ("good news") and *angellein* (to bear a message," "bring the good news of," "announce, proclaim, report, command").[27] Evangelism verbally proclaims the truth and love of Jesus Christ, which is always good news. It communicates who Jesus Christ is and what he is offering us, redemption. This good news is that God is for people and not against them and that those far from God are not subjects of his wrath but are objects of his love.

Pre-Christian Use of Gospel (*Euangelion*)

While in its purest definition the word *gospel* or *euangelion* does mean good news, to tell the good news, or the bearer of good

---

23. Schaal, "Intentional Engagement," 38.
24. Lust, Eynikel, and Hauspie, *Greek-English Lexicon of the Septuagint*.
25. Chan and Carson, *Evangelism*, 15.
26. Dubose, *God Who Sends*, 115.
27. Barrett, *Evangelize!*, 79.

news, the word also had other meanings for the original audience that both Jesus and the apostles spoke to. The word did not originate with the birth of Christianity or at the appearance of Jesus in Jerusalem. Here are three pre-Christ examples of how the word *euangelion* is used to describe good news.

> In 1st Century BC, we see Cicero using the word to describe good news in a couple of his letters to Atticus.
> "First, a trifle please for good news(εὐαγγέλια). Valerius has been acquitted with Hortensius as his advocate." Letter to Atticus 2.3.1 (Circa 60 B.C.)

> "Is that So? Does Brutus really say that Caesar is going over to the right party? That is good news (εὐαγγέλια)." Letter to Atticus 13.40.1 (Circa 45 B.C.)

> "Now this terrible message (that rebellion was brewing) was good news (εὐαγγέλια) to Florus; and because his design was to have a war kindled, he gave the ambassadors no answer at all) to their request for assistance in stopping the sedition before it grew)." Josephus Circa 1st Century B.C) Jewish Wars[28]

Euangelion was used in ancient Rome and even earlier in a more political sense. To announce a new proclamation to the empire's subjects, the Romans would post inscriptions on monuments and statues to make an announcement. "In the emperor cult particularly, in which the Roman emperor was venerated as the spirit and protector of the empire, the term took on a religious meaning: the announcement of the appearance or accession to the throne of the ruler. In contemporary Greek, it denoted a weighty, authoritative, royal, and official message."[29] These announcements would be called "the *euangellion* of _____" (insert the leader/emperor they were talking about).

One of the more famous Roman *euangelion* is from 9 BC, memorializing the life of Caesar Augustus. The Priene Inscription reads:

28. Glen, "Pre-Christian Uses Of 'Gospel.'"
29. Fredericksen, "Biblical Literature."

The providence which has ordered the whole of our life. . .has ordained the most perfect consummation for human life by giving to it Caesar Augustus, by sending in him, as it were, a savior for us and those who come after us, to make war to cease, to create order everywhere. . .the birthday of the god [Augustus] was the beginning of the gospel for the world that came by him.[30]

Here it is ascribing to Caesar Augustus the titles of savior and God, and thus this is good news (gospel) that needed to be celebrated and proclaimed throughout all the regions. Essentially, they were communicating that there was a new king on the throne, and he should be seen as God and the world's savior.

So, when Jesus and the apostles used the word *euangalion* (gospel) in their teachings and writings, they were saying that this is good news but also making a statement that caused a revolution. They knew that those they were teaching also knew that the word *euangalion* was a word describing the ascension of a new king to the throne. So, when we talk about the gospel of Jesus Christ, we share the good news that Jesus lived, died, and rose from the grave, paying the ultimate price for our redemption. We now have the good news to share that Jesus has redeemed us so we can enjoy a relationship with God the Father again. However, the gospel of Jesus Christ also states that there is a new King on the throne. Jesus Christ is the Savior of the world (Acts 13:23; Titus 2:13). Jesus Christ is God (John 20:28).

GOSPEL

The Greek word *euaggélion* (εὐαγγέλιον), when translated in the English Bible, appears as "gospel" over seventy-seven times. *Gospel* is a word derived from the Anglo-Saxon *godspell*, denoting "glad tidings" or "good news,"[31] or to announce the good news or to share and proclaim the good news. So, in sharing the gospel, you proclaim the good news. However, the word *gospel* has been seen

30. Davis, "Pre-Christian Uses of 'Gospel.'"
31. Elwell and Comfort, *Tyndale Bible Dictionary*, 547.

to have other meanings as well. Jesus' plan for salvation is generally referred to as "the gospel," which includes the plan of salvation, its doctrines, declarations, and precepts. Later, "the gospel" is understood as teaching the history of Jesus' life, as we have in the Gospels of Matthew, Mark, Luke, and John.

I have noticed that having a limited understanding of the word *gospel* can lead some to think that sharing the gospel involves more than just speaking good news. I shared a simple thought on my social media page a while back that stated:

> "Evangelism is not telling people how bad they are, but telling people how great Jesus is!"

Most people enjoyed the post, but others questioned it. They commented that to participate in evangelistic activities, you must tell people how sinful they are; they need to know how bad they are before they will appreciate how good Jesus is. Of course, I don't agree with this statement, but I do understand the thinking behind the comments. They see *the gospel* as a noun. I agree that *the* gospel is the story of Jesus' life, death, and resurrection, how he gave his life as a ransom (payment) for all of humanity's sins. Through accepting Jesus' offer of forgiveness (redemption), we no longer are separated from God but can now have a living and loving relationship with God the Father.

However, *evangelism* or *gospel* needs to be read as a verb, as in to proclaim, speak, share, or tell the good news. This does not mean we must tell someone everything we know about Jesus and the Bible for it to be considered evangelism. Francis Dubose states: "When we share the good news, we are gospel-izing or good news-izing. I know this is not good English, but it makes sense in Greek, the original language of the New Testament."[32] So if evangelism is proclaiming the good news of Jesus Christ to non-Christ-followers, why is this practice almost nonexistent among many Christians? I want to suggest that the reason we do not see the activity of evangelism being practiced among Christ-followers

---

32. Dubose, *God Who Sends*, 115.

has more to do with what Christ-followers think evangelism is. In my research, I have learned that Christians are interested in telling their family, friends, coworkers, classmates, and neighbors about the redeemed life they have found in Jesus Christ. But they are not interested in telling people how bad, evil, or lost they are. What if the church saw evangelism through the lens of telling people how good Jesus is instead of the lens of telling people how bad they are? After all, telling people how good Jesus is—sharing his truth, hope, and love with others—is the gospel! Now, I am not arguing that we should never share what separates us from God, the act of sin. After all, the reason that Jesus came to earth was to take care of the sin problem. I am stating that evangelism is much larger than sin; it declares the glory and greatness of King Jesus!

Can the word and practice of evangelism be redeemed? My answer and belief is, *yes!* I have attempted in this chapter to redeem evangelism and put it back into service, defining its original meaning and purpose. I outlined that the church's current context has different definitions and understandings of the word *evangelism*. Even Jesus and the apostles used the word *euaggélion* to make two different but complementary statements. The good news is that Jesus came to give his life as payment and for the redemption of all humankind. They also stated, "There is a new King on the throne." In later chapters, I will share ways to understand and share the gospel with the people you do life with. But for now, redeem evangelism in your life by sharing with people the good news that you have a new King sitting on the throne of your life, and his name is Jesus! Tell people how good he is by simply telling your story as instructed in Psalm 107:1–2. That is evangelism!

3

The Anatomy of Mission

There is a common question I get when telling people that I was raised in the Jehovah's Witnesses religion and now I am a Christ-follower. "What scripture or what gospel tract, sermon, etc. was shared with you that convinced you to leave your family's religion and put your faith in Jesus?" This is asked because while most people do not know all of what the Jehovah's Witnesses believe, they do know that they have strong convictions and that their entire identity is based on their religious beliefs. I also think people ask me this because they are hoping to hear of the quick and easy way of sharing Jesus with people of other faiths. My answer to this question is often met with confusion and disbelief. I say, "I do not remember one certain scripture or gospel tract or even a sermon that convinced me to put my faith in Jesus. While I had many who shared scripture with me, none stands out as the bullseye aha passage. I did have some share different gospel literature with me, but honestly, I do not remember any of them."

> My conversion story was a process that took over eleven months and included more conversations than I can remember.

It took more than just my ears hearing information to lead me to decide. First, there was my mind; my thinking began to change because of the many conversations I had with my classmates. I would process the information they were sharing with me and then try and justify that with what I was taught in my religion. Little by little, my mind and thinking began to change. Then there was my heart. I remember sensing a change that came over me as I started processing these new truths I was learning. No longer was my heart hard to the things I was learning in the Bible. I began to have a heart change for people as well, which affected my eyes. I began to see life and people differently. I began to look at and take note of how Mike and his brother, Jay, treated each other, and how they loved and respected their parents. I saw how Tracy and her sister, Cindy, would act and treat each other at school. Their lifestyle, the way they lived, was consistent with biblical principles. They, too, allowed their faith to dictate every aspect of their identity. Mind you, these were just high school students, fifteen, sixteen, and seventeen years old. None of them were theology experts. But they lived out their faith openly. While neither of their families were perfect, what I saw was two Christian families living with a peace that I could not explain. I never witnessed this peace in my own family, nor did I witness this with anyone in my faith practice. All of this led me to boldly and confidently declare with my mouth that "Jesus is Lord!" That was my response to Tracy when she asked me, "What are you going to do about your faith?"

In the previous chapters, I have defined evangelism as intentionally engaging others in spiritual conversations that can lead to sharing the gospel. I even made the argument that with the many different definitions there are for evangelism, it most definitely has a verbal aspect, as in good news that needs to be shared. The purpose of writing this book is to equip the Christian church of today to engage in more spiritual conversations. I am confident that the more we see Christians speaking the good news of Jesus Christ in their circles of influence, the more we will see people embracing the beauty of the gospel and putting their faith in Jesus Christ. Or, to say it differently, to see more Christians opening up their mouth and telling others about Jesus, and those people say yes to Jesus! Every Christian should engage non-Christ-followers in spiritual conversations, hoping it will lead to sharing the gospel.

MISSION OF GOD

You may be asking, "What is the mission of God?" We must start at the beginning to understand God's mission. Genesis begins by explaining how God created the heavens and the earth and completed the creation process with his most prized creation, humankind. He gave Adam and Eve the liberty to eat from any tree or plant they lay their eyes on, except one. Succumbing to temptation, both Adam and Eve disobeyed God and ate from the forbidden tree. We read of this in Genesis chapter 3. Here, everything changed for humankind. Sin had entered the world, and the separation from God had begun. In this same chapter of Genesis, we read of God's love for his creation, that he declared his plan to make everything right (3:15). This is the first declaration of God's mission to restore the broken relationship with his creation. From that point on, through every book of the Bible, we see God fulfilling that mission. God is a missionary God, and the Bible is our mission manual. The thread of God's mission can be seen from the Pentateuch to the historical books, the books of poetry, and the wisdom books through the major and minor prophets. Then, in the New Testament, we read of God sending his one and only Son to crush the head of the enemy, Satan, by dying for all of humankind's sins and conquering death by rising from the dead on the third day. The Gospels (Matthew, Mark, Luke, and John) detail these events, as well as each, in their own way, recruiting Christ's followers to join God in his mission.

God's mission will not be complete until we are all united together with Christ in heaven. God's desire is that all humankind have an opportunity to be a part of that gathering. Peter tells us, "The Lord is not slow in keeping his promise, as some understand slowness. Instead, he is patient with you, not wanting anyone to perish, but everyone to come to repentance" (2 Pet 3:9). This is where we are invited to join God in his mission. The word *commission* is a compound word meaning common mission. Christians are invited and expected to participate in the common mission, the Great Commission. Joining these two words encapsulates a more specific meaning. As Christ's followers, we have a common passion (compassion), to see all come to repentance. The common mandate (commandment) is to love the Lord our God with our hearts, souls, and minds (Matt 22:37). As a body of believers, we live in a community; our common unity is our relationship and love for Jesus.

So what is this common mission or mission of the church? Missiologist Paul Hiebert says it like this: "The mission of the church is to bear witness to what it now believes. It is to point to, report, and affirm a new reality that stands over against other realities... it is simply telling others the message it has received."[1] Sherwood Lingenfelter defines kingdom work as both "good news and a healing touch."[2] And Charles Van Engen states: "Mission is the people of God intentionally crossing barriers from church to non-church, faith to non-faith to proclaim by word and deed the coming of the kingdom of God in Jesus Christ."[3] I really like Van Engen's definition. Here is how I break down his definition and meaning:

- People of God: Christian church body and/or individual Christ-followers
- Intentionally: Intentionality is key. It is participating on purpose, strategic activity that is done deliberately.
- Crossing barriers: Doing whatever it takes to engage people. Overcoming personal and or physical barriers to reach those far from God.
- Church to non-church, faith to non-faith: Understanding our target audience are those outside the church who have no faith in God at the present time.

1. Hiebert, *Transforming Worldviews*, 285.
2. Lingenfelter, *Leading*, 34.
3. Van Engen, *Mission on the Way*, 26.

SPEAK GOOD NEWS

- <u>Proclaim by word</u>: Verbally speaking out the gospel using words. Would also include using the printed page.
- <u>Proclaim by deed</u>: Demonstration of the gospel as in social justice, discipleship, creation care, etc.
- <u>Coming of the kingdom of God in Jesus Christ</u>: The good news of Jesus' invitation to become citizens of his kingdom, the gospel!

The mission of the church flows from the mission of God. It is not so much that the church has a mission as that God's mission has a church.[4] The mission of the church (*missio ecclesia*) can be seen as living out a life of the Great Commandment (love God; love others) and the Great Commission (make disciples and preach the good news) (see Appendix A).

Our love for God causes us to love what he loves, which is his dear creation, all peoples from all nations. In the Sermon on the Mount, Jesus reminds us that we are both salt and light (Matt 5:13–16). Salt brings healing, and light illuminates the truth. Salt by itself is useless unless applied.[5] It has many uses, including preservation from decay and healing. Things remain hidden in darkness, but the light exposes the truth.[6] The church is salt in that we serve as a healing agent to an ailing world. We are light when we expose the darkness by illuminating the light of the gospel when we share it with others. Salt could be seen as good deeds, and light as evangelism. The love of God then compels us (2 Cor 5:14) to become a disciple or apprentice of Jesus,[7] which provokes us to make disciples and proclaim, tell, share, and preach with others what we have experienced.

If all aspects of mission are considered evangelism or equal to evangelism, then evangelism loses its meaning and significance. The analogy here is that if everything is holy, then nothing is holy.[8]

4. Wright, *Mission of God*, 62.
5. Eberhard, *Salt and Light*, 9.
6. Eberhard, *Salt and Light*, 12.
7. Willard, *Omission*, 2.
8. Larsen, *Evangelism Mandate*, 13.

Again, evangelism (verbal proclamation of the gospel) is just one aspect of the church's role in mission. The verbal proclamation of the gospel is the area of mission that I see needs to be strengthened in the churches across the USA.

OUR COMMON MISSION

I have heard some argue that the mandate on Christians is not so much evangelism but making disciples. The Great Commission is about making disciples of Jesus Christ, teaching them to obey everything that Jesus has commanded. This belief is that some are called to evangelize, but all are called to make disciples. How about you? Do you see evangelism and making disciples as two distinct disciplines? Take a moment and think about that question; what have been your thoughts on evangelism and making disciples? Before I answer that question, it would first do us well to examine the meaning of the Great Commission. The Great Commission is recorded no less than five times, once in each of the first five books of the New Testament. The most known recording of the Great Commission is the one we read at the end of Matthew's Gospel:

> [18] Then Jesus came to them and said, "All authority in heaven and on earth has been given to me. [19] Therefore go and make disciples of all nations, baptizing them in the name of the Father and of the Son and of the Holy Spirit, [20] and teaching them to obey everything I have commanded you. And surely I am with you always, to the very end of the age. (28:18–20)

Matthew's recording comes with a statement, an assignment, and a promise. Jesus has been given all authority. Nobody has more authority in heaven or on earth than Jesus. He assigns us to go and make disciples, baptize people into the triune Godhead, and teach these new disciples to obey all of Christ's commands. And the promise is that he will be with us always as we go and make disciples. This is the great common mission! Making disciples is the process of teaching, learning, and following the ways of Jesus Christ. It is a spiritual journey where we, as Christ's followers, seek to emulate his teachings and character. This is an ongoing process where we begin to look more like Christ each day as we embody his teaching and example. Some ask, "Where is evangelism in the Great Commission"? Many well-meaning Christians think of discipleship as the desired outcome of attending Sunday school, listening to the preaching of God's Word, or by personal Bible study. They see discipleship as an assignment for and to those who already believe in Jesus. Pastor Kevin and Sherry Harney remind us that "Discipleship happens every time one believer takes the hand of another and helps them move closer to Jesus. We can even disciple a person before they put faith in Jesus."[9] This was my experience.

When Mike and Tracy, as well as many other of my Christian classmates, engaged me in spiritual conversations, and they would ask me questions and explain their understanding of Jesus' story, they were, in fact, discipling me. Yes, discipling happens prior to a person putting their faith in Jesus. I see it this way.

 Evangelism is discipleship in utero!

Before someone puts their faith in Jesus Christ, they, at some point, were communicated to by someone or something that planted the seed of faith. Over time, that seed grows. Gestation periods differ in the animal kingdom. It takes humans roughly nine months to gestate life, cats and dogs between fifty-eight and sixty-eight days. Rabbits only take about one month, while elephants can take up to twenty-two months. While time frames may differ, they all result in a birth. Evangelism is discipleship in utero; seeds are planted, nourished, and exercised as we continue to engage in spiritual conversations with non-Christ-followers until that person becomes "born again." When they are born again—the moment they declare Jesus as Lord and start following him as the leader of their life—discipleship does not start; it only continues.

---

9. Harney and Harney, *Organic Disciples*, 22.

Gestation periods in the spiritual kingdom also differ, depending on the person. Some hear the truth of the gospel and right away say yes to Jesus. Others may take weeks, months, or even years to be born again. It took me close to eleven months from initially hearing the gospel for me to say yes to Jesus. How about you? How long was your spiritual gestation period? I thank the Lord constantly that my friends did not give up on me after I rejected what they shared with me many times. They took me by the hand and led me closer to Jesus with each conversation.

While Mathew's recording of the Great Commission is probably the most known, the other Gospel writers and the book of Acts also contain a record of the Great Commission that we can cross-reference and see the evangelism verbal proclamation thread mentioned. Mark 16:15 reads, "He said to them, 'Go into all the world and preach the gospel to all creation.'" Luke 24:47 reminds us that the gospel needs to be preached in his name to all nations, beginning at Jerusalem. In both verses the Greek word *kerysso* is used for "preach," which means to proclaim, herald, or communicate.[10]

John reminds us that as God the Father had sent Jesus into the world to fulfill his mission, Jesus is sending us (John 20:21); it is our common mission. What is that mission? Acts' account of the Great Commission says this: "But you will receive power when the Holy Spirit comes on you, and you will be my witnesses in Jerusalem, and in all Judea and Samaria, and to the ends of the earth" (Acts 1:8). A witness shares what he or she has seen or experienced with another. We, who have our own story and testimony of witnessing and experiencing the truth and love of Jesus Christ, are to tell others, from our current location to the ends of the earth.

ANATOMY OF SPEAKING GOOD NEWS

As outlined above, evangelism is just one aspect of God's mission. Unashamedly, I have made the point that evangelism, or speaking

---

10. Soanes and Stevenson, eds., *Concise Oxford English Dictionary*.

SPEAK GOOD NEWS

good news, requires the use of one's verbal skills. It is communicating by word the good news of Jesus Christ. It is telling others of the hope and new life you have found in Jesus Christ and showing them where they, too, can find this life. While evangelism will always have a verbal component, it would be foolish to think that our mouths and tongues are the only body parts we need to employ. Remember, speaking good news is more about a mindset than a method, more about our posture than a program. A holistic approach in our evangelism activities is needed to be effective. How we think, see, hear, and feel will empower the words that we are sharing.

Mind

The Bible says, "The god of this age has blinded the minds of unbelievers so that they cannot see the light of the gospel that displays the glory of Christ, who is the image of God"(2 Cor 4:4). That means that at one time your mind and mine were blinded to the fact that Jesus is Lord. The god of this age, Satan, did, in all his power, confuse us in not being able to understand the gospel. But Jesus healed us from that, and his light shone through, and we then were able to say yes to Jesus. We need to be convinced in our own mind of the biblical truths about what it means to be a Christ-follower. Here is a short list of fundamental truths we should be confident of:

- God created us so we can worship him and have fellowship with him (Genesis 1).
- God's creation rejected and disobeyed his instructions, causing the relationship to be separated, leading to death, both physical and spiritual (Genesis 3).
- God's love for his creation led him to send his son Jesus to pay the ultimate price to solve the relationship problem (John 3:16).

- Jesus did not just die in our place, but he conquered death and is alive today as a testimony that we, too, can have new life in him (John 10:10).
- Jesus alone is the only way to the Father (John 14:6).
- We only need to look to Jesus and believe in our hearts that he is the Savior, and we will have eternal life (John 6:40).
- Then we can follow the leading of the Holy Spirit, who will guide us in all truth (John 16:8; 13).

We need to continue studying and learning as much as possible about Jesus and his kingdom. We do this first for our own edification and our desire to grow closer to Jesus. We also do this so we will be able to answer the questions that those we are engaging may ask us. Understanding the bulleted points above will ensure that you will always be able to give an answer to everyone who asks you to give the reason for the hope that you have (1 Pet 3:15). However, we keep learning so we can help others with the truth we have learned. When engaging in evangelistic activities, we must engage our minds.

Heart

Belief in the saving power of Jesus Christ means more than just having some intellectual knowledge or information. It means allowing that knowledge to travel eighteen inches, to take root in your heart, where you begin trusting in no one else but Jesus for salvation. Paul told the church in Rome, "One must declare with your mouth, "Jesus is Lord," and believe in your heart that God raised him from the dead, then a person is truly be saved. For it is with your heart that you believe and are justified, and it is with your mouth that you profess your faith and are saved" (Rom 10:9–10). Pastor Timothy Keller reminds us that in the Bible, the heart is the seat of the mind, will, and the emotions. It's the control center of your life—the things you commit to and trust in. It affects the mind, the will, and what you believe as well as your emotions.[11] This means as we engage others in spiritual conversations, we would do well to engage our hearts in these conversations. It is through the heart that we show compassion for those who are far from Christ. Remember, non-Christ-followers (our mission field) are not objects of God's wrath but are subjects of his passion and love. As we engage our hearts in our evangelistic activities, we will then have compassion for people who are lost, helpless, and harassed as sheep without a shepherd (Matt 9:36).

Hands

In the book of James, we are challenged by the acts of service we ought to do for our fellow man. James asks, "Suppose a brother or a sister is without clothes and daily food. If one of you says to them, "Go in peace; keep warm and well fed," but does nothing about their physical needs, what good is it?" (2:15–16). Our acts of service are not to be confused as being the same as evangelism. But our lack of serving our fellow man in times of need is a sign that the gospel is not living in us. Pastor Kevin and Sherry Harney say it this way: "Our compassion and merciful ministry in the world prepare a place for the gospel to be proclaimed, but it still needs to be proclaimed."[12] The acts of service we do in light of the gospel living in us will open the door for proclamation. Jesus appointed the disciples (Luke 9) and the seventy-two followers (Luke 10) to do two things, to heal and to proclaim. As we serve our fellow man, doors will swing open for us to proclaim the name of Jesus. In the story of the Good Samaritan in Luke 10, whom do you think would be the most effective in proclaiming Jesus to the man who was robbed, beaten, and left for dead? I assure you, the priest and the Levite would not be nearly as effective as the Samaritan.

---

11. Keller, *Preaching*, 158
12. Harney and Harney, *Organic Outreach*, 60.

Feet

In the 1989 movie *Field of Dreams*, starring Kevin Costner, Costner's character, Ray Kinsella, while walking through his Iowa corn field, hears a whispered voice say, "If you build it, he will come." This is often misquoted as, "If you build it, they will come." Sometimes, churches take this approach, thinking that if they have a great facility or build a wonderful program, people will naturally just come. Now, there is nothing wrong with great facilities and wonderful programs. However, when we individually participate in evangelistic activities, we are called to *go*. I often hear the saying, "The first two letters in *gospel* are GO—we are to *go!*" As mentioned earlier in this chapter, Matthew's Great Commission starts by saying, "*Go* and make disciples . . ." We must be willing to go to the people who need to hear the truth and love of Jesus. Romans 10:13–15 reminds us:

> [13] . . . "Everyone who calls on the name of the Lord will be saved." [14] How, then, can they call on the one they have not believed in? And how can they believe in the one of whom they have not heard? And how can they hear without someone preaching to them? [15] And how can anyone preach unless they are sent? As it is written: "How beautiful are the feet of those who bring good news!"

Some Bible scholars estimate that apostle Paul traveled thousands of miles throughout the Mediterranean region during his missionary journeys. Now, God may not be asking you to travel thousands of miles at this point and time. However, he may ask you to walk across your city, to your next-door neighbor, across your campus, or even across the room. How beautiful are the feet of those who bring good news!

Eyes

We must see non-believers as God sees them, as lost and heading for an eternity separated from God. Believing and now trusting

SPEAK GOOD NEWS

in no one else but Jesus for salvation should result in us seeing those around us in a different light. When we look at those not serving Jesus, we should not see them as the enemy or as us versus them. We should see people the way God sees them. Try a little exercise. The next time you are out in public, at work, school, or at the grocery store, open your eyes and look. Ask God to give you a Godlike perception to see people the way he sees them. I guarantee you, you will never see the unsaved the same way again. You will begin to have a desire to engage these yet-to-be-saved people in conversation.

Scripture reminds us of the importance of using our eyes when engaging in evangelistic activities. Mark tells us, "When Jesus landed and saw a large crowd, he had compassion on them, because they were like sheep without a shepherd. So he began teaching them many things" (Mark 6:34). Illustrating how his followers should see the lost people, Jesus said: "Don't you have a saying, 'It's still four months until harvest'? I tell you, open your eyes and look at the fields! They are ripe for harvest (John 4:35). We are called to join in Jesus' mission of seeking, looking for lost people to share the gospel with so they can be saved (Luke 19:10)

Ears

Stephen Covey states that the most effective communicators are great listeners. Often, we listen with the intent to reply when we should really listen with the intent to understand.[13] When we listen, we earn the right to be heard. This shows the person we are engaging with that we see them as important and worthy to be heard and understood. Jesus did this with the Samaritan woman at Jacob's well (John 4). They were talking about water; she asked him questions, and he answered. She then changed the topic of conversation to worship. Jesus listened and then talked to her about worship. This led the women to see Jesus for who he is: the Savior of the world.

---

13. Covey, *7 Habits*, 235.

We need to engage our ears to hear what is on the heart of those we are speaking good news to. We must listen to understand, not just listen to respond. This will open the door for us to be listen to, as we share about the truth and love of Jesus.

Mouth

"The gospel is news before it is anything else—it is the announcement of what God has done for us in Jesus Christ."[14] We must *speak* forth the truth, using our voice and words to share the truth and love of Jesus Christ to those we see living without him. Using our mouth (words) to tell people about our experience and knowledge of Jesus Christ can be as simple as inviting others to "come see a man," as the Samaritan women did in John 4. It could simply start with offering to pray with someone to begin a spiritual conversation. Jesus said that his followers would be a witness of him (Acts 1:8). A witness tells others what they have knowledge or experience of. We are only expected to share what we know and why we have put our faith in Jesus Christ.

Evangelism, speaking good news, and sharing the gospel most assuredly needs to be done with words. However, as outlined above, it takes our whole being to be truly effective. Be who you are! You understand the fundamentals of what it means to be a Christ-follower, and you live your life accordingly. Now, look at and go to those that God has placed in your life that are not living with the same hope you have. See if they have a need you can meet, and listen to them as you are earning the right to talk with them. And tell them about the hope that you have. They need to hear why you are serving Jesus. Through your words, God will begin to confirm his love for them.

---

14. Harney and Harney, *Organic Outreach*, 59.

4

The Barrier of Sin

A few weeks into Marine Corps basic training, I questioned if I had made the right decision to enlist in this armed service branch. I remember thinking I should have done more research on each branch. Truth be told, two things tipped the scale in the Marine Corps' favor. First, they have the best-looking dress uniforms of all the services—those dress blues project instant honor and respect to anyone earning the right to wear them. Second, the Marine Corps has the much-deserved reputation of being the most challenging branch to become a part of. You don't join the Marine Corps; you earn the right to become a U.S. Marine. As we marched around MCRD San Diego, toward the southern end of the base, I saw the one thing that I thought would disqualify me and keep me from earning the title of U.S. Marine: the Confidence Course.

The Confidence Course, as the name would imply, is meant to create in the character of each Marine recruit the confidence to overcome adverse barriers in fulfilling their mission. There were eleven obstacles we had to master. I knew the Stairway to Heaven would be my downfall. This is a thirty-foot ladder made of logs. You must climb this ladder, throw your body over the top, and climb back down. Oh, and there are no safety nets or ropes if you fall. Then there was the Slide for Life, in which you begin twenty-five feet up in the air and slide down a ninety-foot rope in different positions—hand over hand, prone position, legs first, or any combination that the drill instructor decides. Oh, and all of this is over a pond of water four feet deep. The last obstacle that had to be mastered was the rope climb. This is where you climb up a twenty-foot rope, and when you get to the top, you touch the log and yell out your platoon number. By the time you got to this challenge, you had zero upper body strength to help you. As we approached the Confidence Course for the first time, I noticed something about the other recruits in my platoon; many were just as tense as I was. I knew if I were to fail, I would not be the only one. Looking back, I now find that odd—being happy with the status quo of civilian confidence, if you will.

To my surprise, every recruit in my platoon successfully conquered the Confidence Course after a few tries. While we were a little intimidated by the barrier we had to overcome, some things emboldened our confidence. First, at every apparatus, there was a drill instructor who had mastered the barrier. They would explain in detail what the barrier was and why we needed to overcome it. Second, the drill instructor would give us step-by-step instructions on how to overcome the obstacle. Once I conquered a barrier, I no longer feared it. As a matter of fact, I remember hoping to go back through the Confidence Course again and again. Once I understood the obstacle, as well as how to conquer it, it no longer posed a threat to my confidence.

In the chapters to follow, I will report on the findings of two national studies I helped conduct on understanding the practice and perceptions that the average Christian has as it pertains to intentionally engaging others in spiritual conversations that can lead to sharing the gospel. I will also provide insights on overcoming some of the common barriers Christians allow to keep them from having these conversations. We will see that it is evident from the responses to the national surveys that Christians equate evangelism with sin. At the risk of being misunderstood in the following chapters, let me state right here: sin is *bad*! Sin is what separates us from God. Sin is why Adam and Eve were cast out of the garden of Eden. Our sin is the reason that Jesus came to earth. It is also

SPEAK GOOD NEWS

why Jesus was arrested, beaten, and nailed to the cross. Jesus gave his perfect, sinless life as a payment for *our* sin. There is no getting around the fact that we all have sinned and fallen short of God's purpose for our lives.

I will unpack the results of the national studies in the next few chapters. The prominent finding in both studies was that

> "eighty-five percent of those studied indicated that they allow a barrier that keeps them from engaging in spiritual conversations."[1]

For the purposes of this chapter, I want to share the three top common barriers so we can see they all are connected to the sin issue. The top three barriers Christians allow to stop them from sharing their faith with others are: 1) Not wanting to be pushy, argumentative, or confrontational; not wanting to call people out on their sins. 2) Not feeling that they are holy or good enough to share their faith. 3) Not knowing what to say, without being confrontational or hypocritical.[2]

When it comes to engaging in spiritual conversations with people who do not know Jesus, many Christ-followers lack the confidence it takes even to start a conversation. A common belief is that most Christ-followers do not want to share their faith with others. There is a belief that Christians are anti-evangelism or at least are not very fond of the idea. There are many guesses as to why we do not see Christians sharing their faith. Writing this book is one way I am dealing with this problem. The other way was to conduct a research project to identify exactly why Christ-followers do not share their faith, or speak good news, or even brag about what Jesus has done in their life to non-Christ-followers. I conducted this research as part of my requirements in writing the doctoral dissertation that I completed in 2020 at Fuller Theological Seminary.[3] The other reason was to inform the ministry of

---

1. Every Home for Christ, *Reviving Mission*, 22.
2. Schaal, "Intentional Engagement."
3. Schaal, "Intentional Engagement."

Every Home for Christ USA, in which I served as the U.S. National Mobilization Director. If we were to serve local churches in carrying Christ to everyone, everywhere, in every generation, then we must understand the local churches' practices and perceptions concerning speaking good news. To validate this research, we also partnered with the Barna Group, asking them to conduct similar research on the church in the U.S.[4] We discovered that the findings for both studies were very similar.

OPPORTUNITY

If you were part of the study sample group, I would have posed this question: "How often do you socialize with someone who does not adhere to the Christian faith?" This question was asked to determine Christ-followers' opportunities to proclaim the gospel with people each day. Think about that for a moment. Before you read any further, answer the question:

> How often do you socialize with someone who does not adhere to the Christian faith?

Socializing in this sense would include people you work with or go to school with, people you interact with at the gym, restaurants, or even your neighbors. Do you interact with them daily, weekly, or monthly, or would you honestly say you rarely have such interactions, say less than once a month?

Thirty-six percent of those answering this question in our survey said they socialize daily with non-Christ-followers. Twenty-eight percent socialize at least weekly, while 12 percent said they interact monthly with non-Christ-followers. So, if you are keeping score, 76 percent of Christ-followers interact with a non-Christ-follower at least once a month. Twenty-four percent of those surveyed reported that they rarely or never have social interaction with non-Christ-followers.[5] If you are a part of the 76 percent,

---

4. See Every Home for Christ, *Reviving Mission*.
5. Schaal, "Intentional Engagement," 88.

then the opportunity to share Jesus with others is not a problem. If you see yourself as part of the group that rarely interacts with non-Christ-followers, let me encourage you to look around. Unless you are living in a secluded, controlled environment, the opportunity is there. Getting to know your next-door neighbor or striking up a conversation with your favorite barista, Amazon delivery person, or coworker is a great place to start.

Similarly, by listening to their stories in interviews, I learned of several ways the interviewees socialized with non-Christians: some talked about those they associated with on their job sites or campuses, while others talked about family members or friends with whom they associated. Eighty-seven percent of the interviewees mentioned at least once that they socialize with individuals who are not Christians at least sometimes. This is consistent with the results of the surveys. The results suggest that most Christ-followers have some social interaction with those who do not adhere to the Christian faith. This means that most of those researched have opportunities to engage in conversations, including spiritual conversations, with those that God has put in their lives. How about you? As a means of exercise, think about your life and the people you interact with regularly. It might be helpful even to write out their names. This can start a prayer list where you ask God to open the door to engage them in a spiritual conversation.

Praying for Opportunities

Praying and asking God to open a door or opportunity for you to engage someone in a spiritual conversation is one of the first steps in speaking good news. Research shows that many of you are doing that already. You are already praying for opportunities to share your faith. Only 9 percent of those we researched responded that they do not pray for opportunities to share their faith. Nineteen percent said they have prayed for opportunities, but it is less than once a month. That leaves 72 percent who stated that they pray at least once a month that God would open a door for them to engage a non-Christ-follower in spiritual conversations. Twenty-four percent said they pray at least once a week, and an astonishing 40 percent indicated that they pray daily for an opportunity. One of the main takeaways is that this tells us that the Christian church is *not* anti-evangelism. If 72 percent pray at least once a month for an opportunity to brag about Jesus to someone, that, my friend, is great news.

A simple exercise would be to take the list you made earlier and take it to God. Talking to God about your friend before you talk to your friend about God will embolden you when the opportunity arises. Once you begin praying for opportunities to engage your friends in spiritual conversations, it will be easier for you to follow through when the opportunity comes up.

WILLINGNESS TO SHARE

Engaging people in spiritual conversations can include a great number of things. From explaining the reliability of the Christian faith (why you are trusting in Jesus) to sharing your own faith story, inviting people to a church service, extending hospitality, and offering to pray for them are easy onramps to speaking good news. Our research discovered that over 90 percent of those surveyed responded that they are very willing or somewhat willing to participate in these activities. This, again, is excellent news for the church. How about you? Are you willing to share the reliability of the Christian faith? To explain the reason you have put your faith in Jesus? Are you willing to share your Jesus (faith) story with someone? Pray for someone? Invite a guest to church? If I were to guess, I would say yes, you are willing or somewhat willing to do those things. You are not anti-evangelism. That is why you are reading this book.

CONVERSATIONS INITIATED

The survey answers to the above questions would indicate that the church is pro-evangelism. Since they are praying for opportunities

SPEAK GOOD NEWS

and even willing to engage in spiritual conversations, one would assume that Christians have many spiritual conversations with non-Christ-followers. We did not want to assume, so we asked this question. How many times in the past year did you initiate a conversation about spiritual matters with a non-Christ-follower? Before you read any further, take a minute and think about how you would answer this question:

> Over the last year, how many spiritually focused conversations did you initiate with a non-Christ-follower?

I know this is a difficult exercise, but understanding this may reinforce why you are reading this book.

Here are the results of the national survey when asked the same question. Twenty-seven percent indicated they initiated zero to one conversations over the last year. Twenty-four percent initiated two to three conversations, while 26 percent indicated that they recall engaging in four to nine conversations over the past year. How does your number compare? When you step back and examine these numbers, there is a gap. We are praying for opportunities and even willing to engage others in conversation about our faith, but only a few conversations are happening. Out of the 365 days in a year, 77 percent of the church is initiating less than nine conversations, or approximately one conversation every month and a half.

Did the conversations have a negative result? That was our next question. We asked them about the result of the conversations they had. Twenty-three percent indicated that the person they talked to followed up with more questions. They wanted to continue the conversation, with 28 percent becoming more interested. Thirty-seven percent realized they began feeling more confident in their faith and became more willing to share again. Forty-seven percent said the conversation resulted in them inviting the person they were engaging with to church. This exposes another gap. If we are praying for opportunities and are willing to have conversations, and when we do there are positive results, then why so few conversations? We began to dig a little deeper to find out exactly why Christians lack the confidence to initiate spiritual conversations with non-Christ-followers.

BEHAVIOR MODIFICATION

Up to 60 percent of those studied indicated their barrier as one of the abovementioned top three. Looking deeper into these barriers, it could be said that many Christians see evangelism as changing people's behavior. "If you just stop your sinful lifestyle, God will accept you." Salvation is not about behavior modification! Salvation happens when we respond to the truth and love of Jesus Christ, trusting in Jesus alone for salvation. If salvation was about behavior modification, then we must rethink Paul's encouragement to the church in Ephesus when he claimed, "For it is by grace you have been saved, through faith—and this is not from yourselves, it is the gift of God—not by works, so that no one can boast" (Eph 2:8–9).

Looking at people as either sinners or saints is not just a contemporary issue. In the seventh chapter of Luke's Gospel, we are told of a time when Jesus was invited to Simon's home to have a meal with other religious leaders. In today's context, we can say that a prominent church pastor asked Jesus and other leaders to a dinner party. As all the church leaders are together talking with Jesus, a woman shows up. Not just any woman; the Bible describes her as a "sinner." We don't know her sin issues, but we know that she has a reputation, for the other leaders know her well (maybe too well). She comes in and falls at Jesus' feet. With her tears, she washes Jesus' feet, and then anoints his feet with an alabaster flask of ointment. Here we are let into the thinking of the religious leaders. "When the Pharisee who had invited him saw this, he said to himself, 'If this man were a prophet, he would know who is touching him and what kind of woman she is—that she is a sinner'" (Luke 7:39). These leaders are focused on behavior! She is a sinner! "Jesus, if he were any kind of prophet, would not let this woman

SPEAK GOOD NEWS

touch his feet." While the religious folks are focused on behavior, Jesus focuses on her faith and the action that her faith has taken.

Jesus illustrates to Simon and the other leaders that his mission is to come and forgive man's debts, and those with larger debts will most likely be more appreciative. Then he turns his back on the religious leaders and looks at the woman. As he continues to talk to Simon and the others, he illustrates how this woman has shown her reverence to Jesus, washing his feet, anointing them, a way of acknowledging her need for Jesus in her life. The story continues, "Then he turned toward the woman and said to Simon, "Do you see this woman? I came into your house. You did not give me any water for my feet, but she wet my feet with her tears and wiped them with her hair. [45] You did not give me a kiss, but this woman, from the time I entered, has not stopped kissing my feet. [46] You did not put oil on my head, but she has poured perfume on my feet. [47] Therefore, I tell you, her many sins have been forgiven—as her great love has shown. But whoever has been forgiven little loves little" (vv. 44–47). Jesus offers her forgiveness for her sins. We read that she receives forgiveness because of her faith, not because she promised to change her behavior or lifestyle. Jesus tells her, "Your faith has saved you; go in peace" (v. 50). Her faith has saved her—not changing her behavior, not by works! If you have believed that in order to *speak good news*, to participate in sharing the truth and love of Jesus with others, your ultimate goal is behavior modification, be free today!

Change should and will be a natural byproduct or next step as a person starts following Jesus. Scripture tells us that ". . . if anyone is in Christ, the new creation has come: The old has gone, the new is here" (2 Cor 5:17). As the Holy Spirit takes up residency, we read it is his job to convict humankind of sin and to lead Christ's followers into all truth and righteousness (John 16:13). In other words, as pastor Craig Groeschel says, "Christianity has never been about behavior modification; its about life transformation."[6] This takes place as a believer yields to the leading of the Holy Spirit. This is part of the Holy Spirit's job description. Author Bob Goff

6. Groeschel, *Winning the War*, 57.

says, "Telling people what they should want turns us into sheriffs. People who are becoming love (thats us) lose the badge and give away grace instead. Tell the people you meet who they're becoming, and trust that God will help people find their way . . ."[7] Goff is encouraging us to love people, to live and walk in grace; the same grace that saved us will save them.

Sin Doesn't Make Us Bad

We are first introduced to the nature and effects of sin in the book of Genesis, where God instructs his creation how to live in the garden of Eden. He makes this one rule: "And the Lord God commanded the man, "'You are free to eat from any tree in the garden; but you must not eat from the tree of the knowledge of good and evil, for when you eat from it you will certainly die" (Gen 2:16–17). "If you disobey me (sin), the price is death." He did not tell them they would become bad if they ate of the tree. No, the effects of sin are much worse; it causes death. Now, we know that Adam and Eve ate fruit from the forbidden tree. We also know they did not die physically, but were dead! Many Scripture passages would support the fact that sin does not make you bad; it makes you dead. One of the more popular New Testament references is Romans 6:23, "For the wages of sin is death, but the free gift of God is eternal life in Christ Jesus our Lord." Jesus claimed his purpose for coming to earth was to provide life for dead people. John 10:10: "The thief comes only to steal and kill and destroy; I have come that they may have life, and have it to the full." He told the Samaritan woman at the well, "If you knew the gift of God and who it is that asks you for a drink, you would have asked him and he would have given you living water" (John 4:10). Then there is the parable of the Prodigal Son. When the son returns from squandering his life in sin and evil, we see the response of the father: "But the father said to his servants, 'Quick! Bring the best robe and put it on him. Put a ring on his finger and sandals on his feet. [23] Bring the fattened calf and

---

7. Goff, *Everybody, Always*, 32.

kill it. Let's have a feast and celebrate. [24] For this son of mine was dead and is alive again; he was lost and is found.' So they began to celebrate" (Luke 15:22–24). Paul explained it to the church in Colossae this way: "When you were dead in your sins and in the uncircumcision of your flesh, God made you alive with Christ. He forgave us all our sins, having canceled the charge of our legal indebtedness, which stood against us and condemned us; he has taken it away, nailing it to the cross" (Col 2:13–14).

In the first chapter of James, the apostle outlines the effect of sin. "When tempted, no one should say, 'God is tempting me.' For God cannot be tempted by evil, nor does he tempt anyone; [14] but each person is tempted when they are dragged away by their own evil desire and enticed. [15] Then, after desire has conceived, it gives birth to sin; and sin, when it is full-grown, gives birth to death" (Jas 1:13–15).

> Sin does not make people bad, it makes people dead!

The truth is that, at times, dead people do bad things. It is also true that, at times, people who have found new life in Jesus Christ also do bad things.

See Dead People, Not Bad People

What if we saw our role in speaking good news not as one of telling people how bad they are (behavior modification) but as one of telling people where to find life? People are searching for life. They are searching for meaning and purpose. The problem is that many people search in the wrong places as they try to fill their lifelessness with anything that might give them life. And we label them as bad! What if we saw people through the lens of the fictional character Cole Sear, played by a young Haley Joel Osment in the 1996 film *The Sixth Sense*. When he saw people, he said, "I see dead people! . . . Walking around like regular people. They don't see each other. They only see what they want to see. They don't know they're dead."

Why do dead people do bad things? They don't know they're dead! That is why Jesus came; to give us life, eternal life. John 5:21 reminds us, "For just as the Father raises the dead and gives them life, even so the Son gives life to whom he is pleased to give it." If we saw people as dead instead of bad, we would not face the pressure of being pushy or confrontational. We would not be calling people out on their behavior but calling people to life.

MY BROTHER KERT

I realized this truth in the late 1980s when I first shared my faith with a non-Christian. I had been serving Jesus for a while now and was anxious to let people know where I had found peace and joy and where I had found life. While visiting my brother Kert and his wife, Julie, I began to share with Kert how my life had been changed by letting Jesus lead it. Kert is my oldest brother; like myself, he was raised in the Jehovah's Witnesses religion. So, in talking with Kert, I knew I was talking with someone with a shared faith background. Kert, like me, was kicked out of the Jehovah's Witnesses for not following their rules. Where I found faith in Jesus right away, Kert did not. He was a very spiritual man who had gone from one form of faith to another, wandering and searching for truth. I love talking to people who are searching.

I shared with Kert how I had allowed Jesus to lead my life. He had many questions concerning some of the Jehovah's Witnesses teachings we were raised with. I tried to answer his questions, acknowledging that I was still learning and growing as a Christian. I did not have all the answers, but I knew where I had found life, peace, contentment, and purpose. We talked about Jesus for about forty-five minutes. To this day, it ranks up there as one of my favorite talks with my big brother. When we were finished, Kert said, "David, you have shown me that Jesus is truly the Savior of the world. You have convinced me that many of the teachings we were raised with are wrong, and Jesus is the answer." Let me tell you, I

SPEAK GOOD NEWS

was so excited to hear his confession. That led me to ask him, "Kert, what do you want to do about this new truth you learned today?" (Remember, that is what Tracy asked me, so I said the same thing.) His reply shocked me. He said, "Nothing!" I was a little confused; I asked, "What do you mean, 'nothing'?" He went on to explain, "David, I am not ready; I am not there yet." I said, "Not ready for what?" He replied, "I am not ready to give up my marijuana yet!" I remember this moment like it was yesterday because I felt as if I was having an out-of-body experience. While I knew that Kert, a child of the 1970s, was a regular user of marijuana, I was a little surprised to hear that he was still using it. In my clean-cut U.S. Marine mind, I remember thinking, "What? Why are you still using marijuana? Dude, you got to stop that! You are married and have two beautiful little daughters. Time to grow up, man!" That is what was going through my mind. However, what came out of my mouth was a teaching moment for both Kert and me.

I said (without thinking), "Kert, where in our conversation did I say that you had to give up your marijuana in order to say yes to Jesus, in order to confess Jesus as your Lord, and allow him to lead your life?" His response was, "Come on, David, I can't be a Christ-follower and still smoke pot!" Then I asked, "Why do you think that?" He continued to share his shortcomings, and said that once he got his life together, he would invite Jesus in. I realized that even non-Christians see evangelism and or coming to faith in Jesus Christ as behavior modification. I went on to explain to him that he would never be able to get his life together without Jesus. He needed to invite Jesus in and allow Jesus to lead and guide him. He asked me how to do that, and I said, "Tell Jesus! You know how to pray; tell Jesus that you believe he is the Savior of the world, and you want him to be the Lord, leader of your life . . . simple." Kert prayed that back to Jesus.

About two weeks later, I received a call from Kert. He said, "David, I flushed it all down the toilet!" I asked what he was talking about, and he said, "My marijuana; all of it is gone." I was surprised and excited at the same time. I had no power or ability to correct my brother's behavior. As Scripture tells us, it is the work of the Holy Spirit in our lives to convict us of sin (John 16:7–14). My brother found life in Jesus Christ. It was not of works, by him achieving some level of holiness first. He found life by putting his faith and trust in Jesus Christ. Kert and his wife connected with a local church. He played drums on the worship team and continued to live his life as a follower of Jesus. Now, truth be told, Kert had episodes where he returned to desiring to smoke marijuana. This does not mean that he was not a servant of Jesus, or that he lost his salvation. He was still trusting in Jesus and allowing him to lead his life. It meant that Kert, like all of us, is human; we all have struggles, and with the leading of the Holy Spirit, we can put to death the sinful nature. While Jesus had put to death all of Kert's sin, he, like all Christians, did not always live in that reality.

As a young Jehovah's Witness, my understanding and motivation for sharing my faith was based on a misunderstanding. I shared my faith because I felt that my salvation depended on it. I think it is also easy for Christians to share their faith with a misunderstanding. We have been led to believe that sharing Jesus with others is to change their behavior somehow; that is why so many evangelism models start by talking about sin. Yes, the issue of sin does, at some point, need to be dealt with. However, I do not believe it has to be in your first conversation with someone. Looking back at my salvation story, I cannot remember a single time when Tracy or Mike ever talked to me about my sin. They both knew me well and could have brought a list of items I needed to repent from. What they did emphasize was the life that Jesus was offering me. They emphasized how much Jesus loved me. This then sparked my interest to want to know more. I have now been serving Jesus for over forty years, and he and I are always working on putting to death my sinful nature. Today, I don't share my faith in Jesus with others because my salvation depends on it; I share because their salvation depends on it.

5

Not Wanting to Be Confrontational

I remember this day in boot camp like it was yesterday. This was the day that our platoon was to tackle the Confidence Course. As I looked around, I sensed that I was not the only one with mixed feelings. On one hand, we were excited to complete this part of our recruit training finally. On the other hand, we were all a little intimidated in not knowing if we could measure up to what we were being asked to do. Each platoon is broken down into squads, and my squad was marched over to our first obstacle of the day, the Stairway to Heaven. This was a thirty-foot ladder made of logs. The object was to climb this ladder, and once you got to the top, you were to climb over the top log, and then climb back down. This was not like a regular ladder; the rungs were made of logs, and each rung was about three feet apart from the next. And to make it a little interesting, there were no safety ropes or nets to save you in the event you lost your balance and fell. Picture this in your mind: about twelve Marine recruits, all looking high up in the air at the top of the obstacle, all of us having a little lump in our throats.

Our drill instructor yelled, "Eyeballs!" (a standard command for you to give the DI your full attention). We all look at our DI. He began instructing us on how to overcome and conquer the Stairway to Heaven. First, he said, "When you are at the bottom, do not look up, and when you are at the top, do not look down." He continued, "All you are doing is moving from one log to a log just three feet away; keep your attention on the task at hand. Just focus on what is right in front of you." While his instructions seemed simple, putting it into practice still seemed intimidating. The first time up, our DI climbed with us. Log after log, he demonstrated what to do. We were then told to climb it by ourselves. Every recruit in my squad successfully conquered the Stairway to Heaven. I remember, after completing the tasks, thinking, "That was not hard at all. As a matter of fact, I want to go again."

JESUS IS OUR INSTRUCTOR

As mentioned in chapter 4, many Christ-followers allow barriers to keep them from engaging non-Christ-followers in spiritual conversations that can lead to sharing the gospel. A common barrier is not wanting to get into an argument or be confrontational with the person you are sharing with. For some reason, many Christians equate evangelism, or sharing their faith with someone, with having to call people out on their sins. At the beginning of this chapter, let me state right here: that is not evangelism! That is not speaking good news. The sin issue needs to be brought up at some point, but calling someone out on their sin is not a prerequisite to sharing your Jesus story. I know evangelicalism has a history of evangelism models, with the believer quoting a list of scriptures or memorizing a script. Most talk about sin right at the beginning, and I respect and honor our rich history of evangelism models. But that is not the only way to participate in evangelistic activities.

Just as I learned to conquer the Stairway to Heaven barrier by listening and watching my DI, the expert in overcoming that barrier, let's turn our attention to the expert in speaking good news, Jesus Christ. We will give Jesus our attention and watch as he demonstrates how to engage someone in a spiritual conversation without being confrontational and argumentative. Let's start with a little exercise. Open up your Bible to John chapter 4. Take a few

SPEAK GOOD NEWS

minutes and read about how Jesus interacted with the Samaritan woman at Jacob's Well. Read verses 1–43. Read them a couple of times if you wish. As you read, note the story's characters, their actions, and any special details that might stand out.

This is one of my favorite stories in the Bible. Each time I read it, I find a new nugget of truth that Jesus is trying to teach me. The protagonists in this story are Jesus and a Samaritan woman. We also see that the disciples and the village people are mentioned. (not the disco group from the 1970s, but citizens of the village Sychar). The story begins by stating that Jesus and his disciples began a journey in Judea, headed to Galilee. The most common route for the Jewish people during this time was to travel around Samaria, which was usually a two-day journey. Yes, they could have just cut through Samaria, which would have saved them much time, but they had a reputation for doing anything to avoid dealing with Samaritans.

Jesus Is Intentional

We read in verse 4 that Jesus decides not to take the normal route but to go through Samaria. Scripture makes a bold statement here; it says he *had* to go through Samaria!

> Why did he *have* to go through Samaria? Because Jesus' passion is intentionally engaging lost people in spiritual conversations.

This was part of his mission coming to earth, to seek and save the lost (Luke 19:10). This was a way of teaching the disciples, and us today, that we need to intentionally look for and seek out lost people to share with them the good news of Jesus Christ. As the disciples go into town to buy food, we find Jesus at a water well. There he meets a woman—a Samaritan woman at that. Samaritans and Jewish people were not known to be very friendly to each other. Jewish people tried to avoid them at all costs. Jewish people had a reputation for thinking of themselves as superior to others.

NOT WANTING TO BE CONFRONTATIONAL

They were the chosen ones and the people of God. Samaritans were looked down on as their bloodline was not as pure as the Jews. They were half-breeds at best. So, right away, we see Jesus breaking down any cultural norms, and he asks this woman for a drink of water. Think about your own life. Is there a people group or even a person you try to avoid? Jesus is teaching us the necessity of being intentional.

Again, I suggest his intention was to engage this woman in a spiritual conversation; notice that he begins talking with this woman in a non-confrontational manner. He asks her for a drink. Simple. At this point, she begins to question Jesus. "'You are a Jew and I am a Samaritan woman. How can you ask me for a drink?' (For Jews do not associate with Samaritans.)" (v. 9). Two observations here. First, you will notice that Jesus does not tell her he is a Jew; she just knows. Jesus does not change into something he is not. We need to be ourselves. Second, her comment that the Jews have a reputation for not liking the Samaritans is telling. How do non-Christians feel about Christians? Do we have a reputation for thinking we are better than everyone else? Is that hurting our testimony and ability to engage non-Christians in conversations? Remember, we are not better; we have just found life and want to share with others where they, too, can find life.

Jesus Is Inviting

As we read on, we see that Jesus begins to take the conversation about drinking water in a spiritual direction. After she asks why he, a Jewish man, is asking her, a Samaritan woman, for a drink, Jesus responds with, "If you knew the gift of God, and whom it was asking you for a drink, you would have asked him, and he would have given living water" (v. 10). Jesus came to give us life. Jesus is not talking with a bad woman, just a dead one. Here we see him inviting her to drink "living water." His invitation takes the conversation in a spiritual direction but is very non-pushy or confrontational. She notices that Jesus had not brought a bucket or cup to drink from, and she tells him so. Knowing Jewish culture, this was

SPEAK GOOD NEWS

a big deal. Jewish people did not share drinking cups with non-Jewish people. To say it plainly, it as an act of racism, not unlike the horrific history of racism in America, where there were separate water fountains for each race. Again, Jesus is communicating to her that he is putting her worth as a Samaritan at the same level as Jews, saying, "I am willing to drink from your cup." This invitation is the opposite of calling her out on her sin or acting superior.

Jesus tells her she will never be thirsty again if she drinks from the water he offers. Jesus is talking more about spiritual matters. She is ready to receive this and says, "Give me this water that I may not thirst anymore, and have to come to this well and draw water" (v. 15). At this point, she still may not understand what Jesus is trying to communicate. So, to go deeper into his meaning, he asks her to go and get her husband. She responds by telling Jesus that she is not married. Then Jesus looks her in the eye and says, "Yes, I know; as a matter of fact, you have had five husbands, and the man you are living with now is not your husband (vv. 17–18). Now, many would read this and say, "See, he is calling her out on her sin! He is telling her that she has a bad reputation and that she has been divorced not once, but five times, as well as currently living in sin, with a man out of wedlock." Sadly, I have heard well-minded Christians say this and have even heard pastors preach this. However, that is a gross misinterpretation of what is happening here.

In this time period, women had zero rights. A woman could not go to the county courthouse and file for divorce. This means that if she is divorced, five different men have rejected her, discarded her, and communicated to her they no longer loved her. But we do not know if she is divorced, only that she has been married five times. What if she has been widowed five times? Can you imagine the pain and hurt she would feel in burying five husbands? Some would argue that Jesus calls her out on living with a man out of wedlock. It is easy for us to judge and cast accusations. But let's be honest here. If you or I were a single woman living in the Middle Eastern town of Sychar, and someone offered us shelter, we would most likely take him up on it, for it is better than being homeless and living on the dangerous streets.

Jesus is Implicit

What Jesus was telling her was that he knew exactly who she was. He understood her hurts, her pain, her rejection. Jesus was saying,

> "You have been rejected or used by six different men, but I am the seventh man; I am here to restore you or complete you."

At this point, the woman has what I would call her "aha moment." She realizes that Jesus is not just some regular Jewish man but says, "I see that you are a prophet." She recognizes she is speaking with someone she can trust in talking to about spiritual matters, so much so that she turns the conversation to the topic of worship, and asks Jesus his thoughts on worship. Just like the DI's instruction to keep our attention on what was right in front of us, Jesus goes with the new direction of the conversation. Jesus responds by telling her that the hour is coming when true worshipers will worship the Father in spirit and truth and that the Father is seeking such worshipers. Notice her response in verse 25. She says, "I know that the Messiah is coming (the one called the Christ); when he comes, he will tell us all things."

Think about this. The group of people that the "chosen ones," the "people of God" (Jews), would avoid like the plague were seeking and waiting for the Messiah to come. People we encounter daily are interested in spiritual matters! They are looking for answers; they are looking for life. Whom do you find it easy to avoid, thinking they don't care about spiritual matters? Maybe God is asking you to engage them intentionally in a spiritual conversation. Jesus then tells her, "I am he whom you are speaking of!" He is telling her that he is the Messiah she is looking for; he is the one that has come to give her life! Can you imagine the excitement this woman feels?

SPEAK GOOD NEWS

The next scene is telling. Right when this happens, the disciples, who were in town to buy food, show up. And instead of being excited that this woman has received life, and living water from Jesus, they begin to become judgmental. Verse 27 gives us a look at a special detail in this story. It makes the comment that no one says anything, which makes us believe that nonverbal communication is happening. Maybe it is the judgmental look on their faces, or possibly crossed arms and shaking their heads left to right in disagreement with what they see. Whatever their nonverbal action is, they say, "What are you doing talking to this woman? I can't believe Jesus is alone and talking to a woman, a Samaritan woman." That begs an examination of our own life. Whom would you be shocked to see Jesus talking with? Think about the vilest, most evil person or group you know of. Again, I think Jesus is teaching his disciples that everyone deserves to hear where to find life.

Jesus Is Instructing

We do not know if it is because of the disciples' appearance or because this woman has just found living water for her soul, but she leaves her waterpot and hurries back to her village. At this same time, Jesus begins instructing his disciples on his purpose and mission. The disciples encourage Jesus to eat some of the food they had brought back, and Jesus refuses and says, "I have food you do not know about, and my food is to do the will of the one who sent me and to finish his work." Jesus says that living on mission and doing what God has called us to do is more satisfying than eating a meal. His attention is on the eternal reward of this Samaritan woman. Jesus continues to teach them by using an illustration from agriculture. He talks to them about harvesting a crop and says, "You are waiting for the crop to be ripe." Here is another special detail in the story. He says, "Open your eyes and look! The field is at the peak of ripeness right now." This should be a daily exercise for all of us. We must keep our eyes open, looking for those ripe for the harvest, those who are ready to be intentionally engaged in a spiritual conversation.

The Woman Invites

Simultaneously, another scene is being played out. The woman who has met Jesus at the well is now back in her village. She has so much excitement that she cannot keep it to herself. Now, I want you to take note of her evangelism strategy here. If you are looking for a model or a script to follow, then her next words would be my recommendation. Her words can be considered Evangelism 101. She says, "Come see a man!" This is an invitation to find life. "Come see a man who told me everything about my life. Could this be the Messiah (Christ)? I think so; come check him out yourself" (vv. 28–29). Like Jesus' invitation to drink living water, her invitation is not pushy, argumentative, or confrontational. She does not say, "Hey, all of you dirty, rotten sinners, you need to repent and get your life together and then come meet my new friend Jesus." No, she is only concerned with them experiencing a life-changing encounter with Jesus. Her simple invitation results in one of the largest responses to the speaking of good news in Scripture. The town makes its way out to the well to meet Jesus. I think we can assume that as the townspeople start on their way out to Jesus, this is the point that Jesus tells his disciples, "*Open your eyes*; the harvest is ready," and what the disciples see is dead men/women walking to find life.

We see a process of events happening when we invite people to find life in Jesus Christ. In verse 39 we read that many Samaritans believe in Jesus because of the woman's story. There is power in telling our story. Psalms 107 instructs those of us who have been redeemed by God to tell our story so others will know. When I share my faith story of coming out of the Jehovah's Witnesses religion, it speaks to and encourages many people. Her telling her story causes people to put their faith in Jesus. The second thing that happens in the process is that after her neighbors spend more time with Jesus, they remark in verse 42 that they now have seen and heard Jesus for themselves and truly believe that he is the world's Savior. They now have their own story to share with others.

Our Inference

Now that we have walked step by step with Jesus, following his instruction and example on engaging someone in a spiritual conversation, we can come to some conclusions. Jesus' passion and mission are to seek and save the lost. Jesus intentionally sought out people who needed to hear the good news that he is the Messiah. When he engaged those he sought, he did not start by telling them how bad they were or how disappointed he was in them. He focused on what was right before him: a dead woman needing life. His initial conversation was a common topic, thirst, and he requested a drink. He answered the woman's questions without condemning her. He met her at her deepest need: hurt, pain, and rejection. He offered her living water, and she accepted it. The book of Numbers says that God is not a man that he can lie. He can't change his mind (23:19). So if he offered, and she said, "Give me this water," he must have given it to her. Did you notice in the story that Jesus did not tell her, "Go and try and reconcile with your first husband; then I will give you living water!" or, "First, move out of the home you are living in, with the man who is not your husband, and then you can have this living water!" No, he simply said, "Ask." This, my friend, is evangelism; this is speaking good news! It would be safe to assume that as days passed, this woman began to make changes in her life reflecting her faith in Jesus. She, as the Scripture tells us, became a new creation; the old things passed away, and all things have become new (2 Cor 5:17). She did not have to modify her behavior to accept Jesus, but by accepting Jesus, there became a desire to change.

After I conquered the Highway to Heaven obstacle in the Marine Corps Confidence Course, I wanted to do it repeatedly. Not only did it boost my confidence in what I could do, but it was exciting at the same time. After you intentionally engage someone in a spiritual conversation that can lead to sharing the gospel, you, too, will be full of confidence. It will be so exciting to be a part of someone's redemption story; you will want to do it repeatedly. I trust that letting Jesus guide us in intentionally engaging someone without being pushy or argumentative has now helped you overcome this barrier to speaking good news.

6

Not Feeling Good (Holy) Enough

After successfully conquering THE Stairway to Heaven, the next barrier my squad had to overcome was the rope climb. This thick rope hung from about twenty feet high in the sky. When we reached the top, we were to yell out our platoon number and a loud and healthy, "Oorah!" After using most of my upper body strength to get over the Stairway to Heaven, I dreaded having to call upon my arms and chest muscles again to complete this task. Our DI once again yelled, "Eyeballs," and we gave him our attention as he began to teach us how to make it to the top. First, he grabbed the rope with his hands and started to climb up, hand over hand, until he got about halfway up. He came back down and explained that this was not the correct way to conquer this objective. We needed to learn to use all the strength and skills available to us, not just our hands and arms. He began to demonstrate the proper way to climb this long rope. He jumped up and grabbed the rope with his hands and brought his arms close to his body. He then wrapped the rope around his right leg and had the bottom of the rope cross his right foot. He stepped on the rope with his left foot, grasping it between both feet, anchoring himself, if you will, with his feet acting like a brake. He left off the "brake" and pulled his legs up to his chest, as if doing a reverse squat. He again applied the brake, loosened his hand grip, and stood up. His upper body strength was not being used as much as his legs and lower body. When he got about halfway to the top, about ten feet in the air, he set his brake with his feet and, to my surprise, let go of the rope with his hands. His point was that all of the strength and skills to climb the rope were not in his hands and upper body but in the anchor of his lower body and legs.

One by one, each of us climbed the rope to the top. Using our legs for strength and feet for brakes. Our hands and arms guided the ascent, but the skill and strength came from the lower body. Once we arrived at the fifteen-foot mark, our DI instructed us to get a good hold of the foot brake and then let go with our arms. This was scary, I have to admit, but it worked. When we relied on the correct muscles and parts of the body for the job, the task was easy to overcome. It was exciting to get to the top and yell, "Platoon 1013, oorah, oorah!"

DON'T WANT TO BE A HYPOCRITE

Another common barrier Christians allow to stop them from speaking good news about Jesus to others is the feeling of not feeling good enough and not being qualified to speak to others about their faith. This does not mean they did not know certain strategies, models, or methods. They admitted knowing certain aspects of the popular evangelism approaches their churches used. As I began to go deeper with those I researched in our one-on-one interviews, the word or topic of shame began to surface with many. They expressed that they did not feel they were good or holy enough yet to talk about Jesus to others. They were not ashamed of the gospel of Jesus Christ; they knew it is the power unto salvation. They were ashamed of their representation of the gospel of Jesus Christ. In essence, they did not want to be a hypocrite. They allowed their former or current state of imperfection to keep them from sharing with others the new life they found in Jesus. They believed that to share their faith, they had to reach a certain state of holiness.

SPEAK GOOD NEWS

    This barrier became clear to me as I was interviewing one of the subjects of my study. For the purposes of this story, I will call her "Kate." Kate was in her early forties and was excited about the opportunity to be interviewed for my academic work. Kate attended an incredible church known for its evangelistic culture. The church constantly provided opportunities for its members to serve in many outreaches. At the point of the interview, Kate had been serving Jesus for about a year and a half. I asked her if she participated in the many outreaches that her church offered. She excitedly responded, "Yes!" She even went on to brag about her church and how she felt she had a purpose to be a part of a life-giving organization that served their community. Since my study was on Christians' practices and perceptions regarding speaking, vocalizing, and communicating the good news of Jesus, I asked her this question: "Since you participate in the many outreaches your church provides, can you tell me how you share or speak with people about Jesus that you are serving in the outreaches?" She answered, "I don't!" Not that she did not want to answer my question, but she had no stories to share. She went on to share that when her church had an outreach, she always chose a job or a task that kept her from ever having to talk to someone about her faith. Obviously, my next question was, "Why?"

    Kate began to tell me her life story. She mentioned that she had lived a very sinful life, even noting that her lifestyle had a reputation in the community. She was extremely ashamed of her past. She said that every time the church conducted an outreach, she knew there would be people there who would see her, judge her, and possibly bring condemnation to the church and Jesus. So, she purposefully would serve in functions where she did not have to speak to anyone about her new life in Jesus Christ. She had lived a sinful life and did not feel worthy enough to share about Jesus. Kate allowed her past state of imperfection (death) to keep her from telling others where she found life. Many others I interviewed had similar stories of why they did not speak about the new life they found in Jesus. One man shared that after becoming a Christian, he still struggled with areas of his sinful character. Until he was no longer sinning, he would not bring shame to the name of Jesus by trying to act like he was perfect.

This barrier is self-created in the minds of new or good-hearted Christians. In sharing this barrier with my friend and peer mentor Pastor Kurt Johnston, he reminded me that the church is partially responsible for creating such a belief. He said many churches and youth groups would have those wanting to participate go through an interview process when putting a mission or ministry team together. The hope was to weed out those who were not, say, the good church kids. When Kurt shared this, I was instantly able to relate. As a new believer, I applied to join our church's mission team in England. I was asked to give a short testimony of my walk with Christ, which I did. It took about thirty seconds for the youth pastor to tell me I was not ready to go on a mission trip. I was told, "Maybe next year, David!" I remember feeling like a failure, not worthy of being used by God. No wonder many Christians feel that to share their faith publicly, they must achieve a certain level of holiness. If that were true, my question would be, "How perfect or holy do you have to be?" Maybe you are reading this and have come to the same conclusion. The bottom line for you is simply that you do not share about your new life in Jesus because you do not want to be a hypocrite. You do not want to disgrace the name of Jesus, so you refrain from speaking about him. If that is the case, I pray that God will use the rest of this chapter to set you free from the bondage of thinking you are not good enough to brag about Jesus to others.

A hypocrite claims to be one thing, but is not. The term dates back to Shakespearian times, when actors would be assigned a role in a play. An actor may have multiple parts in the play. They would be on stage as one character, and in the next scene, they would change costumes or even don a mask and come out as a new character. These actors were called "hypocrites." In modern-day vernacular, the term *hypocrite* always has a negative connotation. Nobody wants to be known as a hypocrite. Tanner Peake, the International President of Every Home for Christ, is noted for sharing that

SPEAK GOOD NEWS

> "the people we are sharing with, non-Christians, don't have a problem with evangelism; they do, though, have a problem with hypocrisy."

When we are sharing the good news of Jesus Christ, where we have found life, no one is ever asked to be a hypocrite. This goes back to the misconception that sin makes a person bad, and since I am now a Christian and Jesus has forgiven me of my sins, I should not be sinning anymore. But in reality, I am still struggling in some areas of sin. Therefore, I should not say anything, fearing being labeled a hypocrite. We are not tasked with pretending to be someone we are not. I am convinced that non-Christians respect our testimony more when we are honest and upfront with them, saying, "I have found life and purpose in Jesus Christ. This does not mean I have it all together or am perfect. I still struggle in some areas of my life. But now I rely on Jesus to get me through those times. I find peace and strength as he stands with and walks alongside me daily." Here, we are honest in describing our current situation while bragging about the peace that comes from finding life in Jesus Christ.

As with the first barrier we shared, not wanting to be pushy, confrontational, or argumentative, and not wanting to call people out on their sin, this barrier is connected to sin as well—our own. Remember, sin does not make you bad; it makes you dead. Our mission is not telling people how bad they are but telling people where to find life. As with the last chapter, let's look at how Jesus deals with this issue. To start, we are going to do a little exercise. Open your Bible to Luke chapter 5. This time, I want you to read verses 1–11. This is a short story, so you should be able to read it a couple of times to get to know it well. As before, please take note of the characters, their actions, and any special details that might jump out to you.

"AWAY FROM ME, LORD"

The protagonist in this story is a young Jewish man named Simon. Other characters include Jesus, the crowd of people that Jesus is preaching to, as well as James and John, the sons of Zebedee. We see the actions of each person mentioned as simply going about a normal day. Simon has just finished an unproductive night of fishing and is cleaning and repairing his nets. Not only is Simon there, but his partners, James and John, have finished their fishing shift and have their boat docked near Simon's. Jesus appears and intentionally engages Simon in a conversation, asking if he can use Simon's boat as a place to teach from, as a large crowd presses on him. It would be interesting to note that up to this point in Jesus' ministry, while attracting large crowds, he has no real followers yet. Jesus teaches the crowd, and when he is done, he asks Simon to go fishing. Simon, obviously listening to Jesus preach as he was preaching from his boat, says, "Rabbi, I have fished all night, and there is no fish; I'll get back at it tomorrow." We read that Jesus is insistent, and Simon, a good Jewish boy, relents and gives in to the "rabbi's" request.

We quickly see that his obedience pays off. Simon catches so many fish that his nets begin to break. He calls over his partners, James and John, and they, too, get in on the haul of fish, and their nets begin to break. This is a supernatural catch of fish. Just think of the excitement, not only for Simon, but for James and John. So much fish! I always think, "What if Simon refused Jesus' request? He would have missed out on such a blessing." He allows Jesus to interrupt his day. He is obedient to Jesus' request. If we want to encounter God truly, we need to be prepared for interruptions. The Bible says, "Many are the plans in a person's heart, but it is the Lord's purpose that prevails" (Prov 19:21). God has a habit of interrupting us. Throughout the Bible, we see many examples where God interrupted someone's routine and asked them to change course. In every case, the adjustment resulted in an accomplishment of God's purpose through them.

SPEAK GOOD NEWS

- Noah: God called on him to build an ark, and we all know how that played out. Can you imagine how confused Noah must have felt when God interrupted his life to build an ark in a dry, dry land?
- Abram: Uprooted his entire family and moved from Ur to establish a new nation in Canaan. Today, we call this modern-day Israel.
- Moses: Gave up his comfortable life not once, but twice! The first, he had to give up living in a beautiful palace in Egypt. Then, forty years later as he worked and enjoyed life as a shepherd, he was interrupted to lead the Israelites out of Egypt.
- David: Lived as a shepherd until God promoted him to become an influential king.
- Mary: Just a teen, preparing for her marriage to Joseph. Talk about an interruption!
- Saul (who later became Paul): Experienced a miraculous life change on his way to another city to persecute Christians.

If we are listening, I am confident that we, too, will hear God ask us to do something that may seem like an interruption at the time, but I am convinced it will allow us to encounter him in ways we can only dream of.

This is certainly the case for Simon. Not only is he so impressed and blessed by the catch of fish, but his perspective of who Jesus is changes. Remember, in verse 5, he sees Jesus as "Rabbi" or "Master." But after encountering Jesus' teaching and the supernatural catch of fish, he now sees Jesus as "Lord." This chapter is about overcoming the barrier of not feeling qualified, holy, or good enough to share our Jesus story with others. Please note that this is not a contemporary issue. The issue of sin and not feeling like we measure up is found throughout Scripture. But in this story, we see how Jesus deals with this barrier. After experiencing this catch of fish, not only does Simon's perspective of Jesus change, but the reality of who he is, in comparison to that new perspective, comes to light. In verse 8 we read, "When Simon saw this, he fell at Jesus' knees and said, 'Go away from me, Lord; I am a sinful man!'" I can sure relate to Simon here. He knows his shortcomings, his imperfections, and his sins. In comparison to Jesus, he sees himself as a dirty, rotten sinner!

One thing to note here: it is not Jesus who brings up the issue of sin. It is Simon. Simon acknowledges that he is a sinner. In essence, Simon is saying, "Away from me, Lord. I am not qualified to be in your presence. I am a sinful man and am not worthy to be near you." If Simon had participated in my study, he would have responded that he did not feel qualified. As we read on, we will see how Jesus deals with this issue of not feeling holy or good enough.

JESUS QUALIFIES HIS FOLLOWERS

In verse 10, after Simon acknowledges his sinfulness and unworthy state to be in Jesus' presence, Jesus says something to Simon and us that is telling. Jesus replies, "Simon, don't worry or let that cause you to fear; follow me, and I will make you fishers of people." Simon says, "I don't feel qualified to be in your presence."

> Jesus replies, "Don't worry about that; follow me, and I will qualify you!"

When speaking good news to people, the good news is that we have found life in Jesus Christ; we should not let our former or current state of imperfection keep us from doing so. The Bible tells us that we have all sinned and fallen short of God's glory (Rom 3:23). So if we let our past or current imperfection stop us, nobody would be sharing. As soon as we say yes to Jesus, he invites us to join his mission. We read in verse 11 that when they hear this, they bring their boats in, leave everything, to follow Jesus. Think about that for a moment. They leave *everything*! They leave their boats, nets, families, and the supernaturally large catch of fish. Why? Because when you encounter God—his love, his forgiveness, and the life he offers—nothing else matters!

SPEAK GOOD NEWS

This is the same response the Samaritan women who met Jesus at the well had. Remember, in that story, she left her water pot, ran back to her village, and told everybody about her encounter with Jesus. A couple of things to take note of here. First, Jesus did not tell her *not* to share with other people until she either married the man she was now living with or moved out. He did not tell her that she needed to achieve some level of holiness before sharing. An authentic encounter with Jesus will compel us to tell as many people as possible. Second, she did not allow the reputation she had currently of being a woman who had multiple marriages and one whom the townspeople most likely knew was living with a man out of wedlock to keep her from telling others where to find life. And neither should we!

This does not mean that we should not strive to live holy lives. God has given us the Holy Spirit to lead and guide us in all righteousness. As we are being perfected in the image of Christ, with the help of the Holy Spirit, we attempt to put to death the desires of our sinful nature. While justification happens instantaneously the moment we say yes to Jesus, sanctification, on the other hand, takes time. We are not expected to wait until we are fully sanctified before sharing how we found life in Jesus with others. If we did, it would be too late. Nobody I know is wholly sanctified on this side of heaven. I know I am not as holy or as good as I wish I were.

What helps me when I feel I am not good or holy enough is remembering my DI's instruction as he helped us conquer the rope climb. When I am using my righteousness, something the apostle Paul called "dirty rags," I see that it is like trying to climb the rope using only my upper body strength. We can all go just so far in our own strength. However, the moment we let go, we will fall flat on our faces. We need to learn to see Jesus as our anchor. We brace ourselves, allowing all of our strength and power to come from him. If we anchor ourselves in Jesus, even if we let go or our own strength gives up, we will not fall. I also see this as a promise we read in Matthew's account of the Great Commission. After giving all of us instructions on our common mission, he follows it up with a promise. He says, "And surely I am with you always, to the very end of the age" (Matt 28:20). Jesus is there with us always. We can rely on his righteousness, holiness, and strength.

THE JOY OF OUR SALVATION

Let me provide a closing encouragement for those of you who are new followers of Jesus Christ, and may not feel you have what it takes to speak good news, and for those of you who have been Christians for a while but still don't feel qualified. The night before graduating Marine Corps boot camp, our senior drill instructor, Staff Sergeant Perez, gave our platoon an encouraging send-off. In his short speech, he said something that has stuck with me for all these years. He said, "If I was to have to go into battle tomorrow, and I was able to pick the Marine platoon to lead, I would pick all of you here in Platoon 1013, over a platoon of Marines who have been in the Corps for many years." At first, this was a little confusing. But it was later that I realized what he was saying. Fresh out of boot camp, Marines are what we call "gung ho Marines." I mean, they are ready to fight and do whatever is asked of them. They have a passion to show the world that they are, in fact, a U.S. Marine. Marines who have been in the Corps for a while tend to lose that gung ho spirit. Getting them to want to go to battle may take a little more effort.

    It is similar to serving Jesus. I remember getting excited about going out and sharing my faith when I was a brand-new Christian. One more seasoned Christian commented to me, "Oh, you are in the honeymoon period; that will wear off." As a new believer, like a fresh graduate from Marine boot camp, I was ready to go and share my faith. I am glad my passion for sharing my faith has not worn off. However, if you are reading this and you feel that you have lost that passion at some point, there is a way to get it back. Take comfort from the psalmist David, who found himself in a similar state. The prophet Nathan came to him after David had committed adultery with Bathsheba, and in praying to God for forgiveness and mercy, David also prayed the following in the Psalm 51:

SPEAK GOOD NEWS

> [10] Create in me a pure heart, O God,
> and renew a steadfast spirit within me.
> [11] Do not cast me from your presence
> or take your Holy Spirit from me.
> [12] Restore to me the joy of your salvation
> and grant me a willing spirit, to sustain me.
> [13] Then I will teach transgressors your ways,
> so that sinners will turn back to you. (vv. 10–13)

David prayed for forgiveness and asked God to restore the joy of his salvation. David asked for a willing Spirit to do what God had called him to do. David also understood his call to teach those people who are dead (transgressors) where to find life, and that is in turning to God. That, my friend, is our calling as well. And the promise is that we get to do it with Jesus being with us always as our anchor and our strength.

7

Not Knowing What to Say: Part 1

After completing ten of the eleven Marine Corps Confidence Course obstacles, my platoon faced the final test, the Slide for Life. The objective here is to slide down a ninety-foot rope, which started about twenty feet in the air and gradually ascended to ground level over a pond of water about four feet deep. Again, our DI gave us basic instructions on how to conquer this task. I remember he warned us not to rely only on our hands and arms, as they would give out, and we would end up falling into the pond of water. He demonstrated that there was a process for properly completing the task. We started by laying our body across the top of the rope, utilizing our core muscles to maintain our balance. Once those muscles were tired, we would switch our body position, where we began to hang from our arms and feet—trying to carry most of our weight with our legs and feet. Gradually, we would move down the length of the rope, switching positions and using all of our body's strength. Many of the recruits fell into the water because they relied on just one muscle group to accomplish the task. We were instructed to start over after climbing out of the water pit. You read that right—"we"; I got wet that day. However, understanding that there was a process to follow as we tried to overcome this obstacle was the first hurdle. Putting the process into practice was the key. Each of us, some dry and some wet, conquered the Slide for Life that day; not only the Slide for Life but the entire Confidence Course.

With over two decades of evangelism-focused ministry experience, I am constantly asked how I share my faith, or if I will let them in on my secret in sharing my faith. One request I get more than any other is this: "David, tell me what to say!" I think this is a legitimate request for two reasons. We have been inundated over the last century of evangelicalism with many evangelism programs and methods. With the greatest intentions, these evangelism models train the Christian to use the correct words, illustrations, or scriptures to try and convince non-Christians that they should put their faith in Jesus. I have used many of these models in my ministry, so I see value in them, and in the next few chapters, I will highlight a couple that I use in my own life. However, I feel that this also communicates to Christians that to speak good news to people who are not Christians, they *have* to follow a script or model to be successful. Second, this is a legitimate request because Christians know people that they want to share the good news of Jesus Christ with, and they do not want to mess it up.

AMBASSADORS AND PRIESTS

> Evangelism, or speaking good news, is more about a posture than a program; it is more about a mindset than a method.

As mentioned above, there is nothing wrong with following a program or method in speaking good news. However, having a proper posture and mindset is more important. Understanding our call, who called us, and what we are called to do is essential. The barriers Christians allow in their lives to keep them from engaging in spiritual conversations could be eliminated by having proper posture and mindset regarding speaking good news.

In writing to the church in Corinth, Paul communicates our call as well as who is calling us to speak good news by stating,

NOT KNOWING WHAT TO SAY: PART 1

"We are therefore Christ's ambassadors, as though God were making his appeal through us. We implore you on Christ's behalf: Be reconciled to God!" (2 Cor 5:20). We are Christ's ambassadors! A country sends an ambassador as its highest-ranking official representative to a foreign country. The ambassador represents the head of state, the king, the president, or the prime minister, and is sent to another nation. The United States has over 175 ambassadors deployed across the globe. Those ambassadors represent the government of the United States in those foreign lands. Ambassadors do not speak for themselves; they are the mouthpiece of the nation that sent them.

Paul is saying that we are Christ's ambassadors. Jesus Christ is the head of state. He is sending us from the kingdom of light (kingdom of God) to represent him in the kingdom of darkness. When you know who you are, you will know what to do. So, in God's eyes, you are his highest-ranking official, representing him and his agenda in the location he has placed you. We are ambassadors, and Paul says that God is making his appeal through us. We are to implore people, on Christ's behalf, to be reconciled to God! In this case, the reconciliation is going from death to life. When we engage people in spiritual conversations, we are not speaking from our own agenda or for personal gain. We are communicating to others that we serve King Jesus, who is our Savior, and he is offering life to all who would ask.

To support Paul's teachings that we are called to be ambassadors, Peter takes it a step further and says, "But you are a chosen people, a royal *priesthood*, a holy nation, God's special possession, that you may declare the praises of him who called you out of darkness into his wonderful light" (1 Pet 2:9). Have you ever seen yourself as a priest? That word may conjure up a lot of thoughts in your head. If you are Protestant, you may think the word means something very Catholic. If you are from the Catholic tradition, you may think of those who lead the church. Or maybe the word in our day and age brings feelings of suspicion or distrust. Again, when you know who you are, you will know what to do. According to Jack Hayford, in Latin, the word for priest is *pontifex*, and the original definition of *pontifex* is "bridge builder." It is the root word that some of our English words have been derived from, like *pons*, which means bridge, or *pontage*, the toll we pay to cross a bridge. We also get the word *pontoon*, meaning a floating bridge.[1] This was one of the biggest issues during the Reformation. The reformers saw the priest as more of a barricade to God than a bridge during their time. The priesthood was always meant to be something practical, to help cross over from here to there. So as priest of God's kingdom, we have the kingdom responsibility of bridging the gap for those who need a redemptive relationship with Jesus Christ and connecting them to God. Not only does Peter share what we are called, but he shares what we are supposed to do: "that you may declare the praises of him who called you out of darkness into his wonderful light." This sounds like speaking good news to me.

Living out our faith with the right posture means knowing that God calls us to be his representative, giving us the ministry of reconciliation and that we are representing him everywhere we go. When we have the mindset that we are simply bridging the gap between man and God by declaring the praises of God, barriers begin to break down.

> When you know who you are, you will know what to do!

I have shared stories in the Bible about overcoming two of the top barriers Christians have expressed they allow to keep them from intentionally engaging others in spiritual conversations. First, we shared about the barrier of not wanting to come across as pushy, argumentative, or confrontational, calling people out on their sins. Second, we addressed the issue of not feeling that we are holy or good enough to tell people about Jesus. The third barrier that we will discuss in this chapter is a combination of the first two, which is the barrier of not knowing what to say. When I sat down and interviewed those for my study, they commonly expressed the third barrier like this: "I do not know what to say without

---

1. Hayford, *Worship His Majesty*, 89.

appearing confrontational and/or hypocritical." They understood certain methods, scripts, illustrations, and programs used by many churches. However, they also saw these methods as having to be confrontational, or it caused them to try and express something that they may not have had full victory over yet, sin.

JESUS' INSTRUCTIONS

As with the two previous chapters, I would like us to look at Scripture and see how Jesus dealt with this issue. While there are many examples in Jesus' ministry that we can look to for direction, Luke chapter 10 gives us insight into how Jesus taught his followers to intentionally engage others in spiritual conversations. So, let's start with our exercise. Open your Bible to Luke 10 and read the first twelve verses. Again, this will be an easy read, so read it a couple of times to get to know the story. As you do, please note the different characters mentioned, their actions, and any special details that might pop out to you.

Now, at this point in Jesus' ministry, it is important to note that he has chosen the twelve disciples and has a growing group of followers like you and me. In this story, Jesus once again takes center stage as the protagonist. Other characters include the seventy-two followers, the man of peace and the opposite, the man of no peace, and the Lord of the Harvest, and I would also point out that he mentions sick people. As far as their actions go, Jesus instructs the seventy-two what to do as they go out and speak good news. And here we read of the process that Jesus shares with them. But before we go into each of those actions, I feel it is important to point out a special detail we read at the very beginning. The passage starts out, "After these things..." or "After this..." After what? This would cause us to look at the events in chapter 9. Now, you can read the entire chapter; however, let me bring your attention to its very beginning, Luke 9:1–2. "[1] Then He called His twelve disciples together and gave them power and authority over all demons, and to cure diseases. [2] He sent them to preach the kingdom of God and to heal the sick." As the head of state, Jesus is sending out twelve ambassadors to represent his kingdom. As you read the beginning of chapter 9, you will see many similarities to chapter 10.

In chapter 9, Jesus sends out the twelve (disciples) to minister to others. Two specific areas are to heal and to preach about the kingdom of God. If we only had chapter 9, we could argue that the call to go out and share about the kingdom of God is a task only given to the church's leadership (the twelve). But in our story today, we see that Jesus is appointing a larger group: "After this, he appointed seventy-two others . . ." He is inviting and commissioning all of his followers (ambassadors) to go out and tell people about his kingdom. I also appreciate that Jesus' action here is that he is not just saying, "Go heal and preach!" and leaving us to figure out how to accomplish the task. He gives us instructions, even sharing with us that there is a process.

Necessity of Prayer

Jesus begins by stating two facts. First, the harvest (people) are ready to hear about this kingdom. They are ripe. Secondly, the task is so large that even the seventy-two cannot accomplish the task at hand. So, Jesus says, because the task is so huge, and because the harvest is ready now, pray to the Lord of the harvest to send out more laborers. We need to pray and ask God to activate other believers to join us in the mission of sharing the good news of God's kingdom with others. I see this in one part: a prayer that God will activate myself and others. The thread of prayer is connected to evangelism throughout Scripture.

In the book of Job, we read that Job prayed for his friends (42:10), and God heard Job's prayer on behalf of his friends and blessed them. In Paul's first letter to Timothy, we read Paul encouraging, even exhorting us about the necessity of payer. He shares that we need to pray for "all people" and even points out that this includes kings and people in authority. One purpose for this is so that we can live peaceful lives. However, Paul also connects it to evangelism. "For this is good and acceptable in the sight of God our Savior, who desires all men to be saved and to come to the knowledge of the truth" (1 Tim 2:3–4). Then, in the next few verses, he shares about the kingdom of God by describing the acts of the King, Jesus. Pray for all people, those in authority, those we like and dislike—it does not matter; we need to pray for them. It is much easier to share the good news of Jesus Christ in a time of peace.

Paul also requests prayer for himself as it pertains to sharing the gospel. In Ephesians 6, we read about the importance of putting on the full armor of God: the belt of truth, the breastplate of righteousness, having our feet ready to bring the gospel of peace, followed by the shield of faith, the helmet of salvation, and the sword of the Spirit, the word of God. As a Marine, I would agree that a person wearing that armor is dressed for battle. However, even if we are prepared for battle with all the above-mentioned tools, we are still not ready. Paul says, now that you look ready for battle, start praying. Paul says to pray always with all prayer and supplication (v. 18). Then he requests the type of prayer to pray: "Pray also for me, that whenever I speak, words may be given me so that I will fearlessly make known the mystery of the gospel" (v. 19).

As Evangelist Ed Silvoso is quoted as saying, "We must talk to God about our neighbor before we talk to our neighbor about God.[2]" Prayer is a necessary element in all of kingdom work, especially in the area of speaking good news. This is where we, the ambassadors, contact and communicate with the head of state that has appointed us. As we pray, we begin to have Jesus' heart for lost people; it will help fuel our efforts to implore people to be reconciled to God. This part of the process is happening. According to our research, up to 72 percent of those studied say that they pray for an opportunity to share their faith with a non-Christian.[3] Keep it up; we should include this daily in our prayer list.

---

2. Silvoso, *That None Should Perish*, 256.
3. Every Home for Christ, *Reviving Mission*, 53.

SPEAK GOOD NEWS

Go with the Shepherd

As we continue in our story, after we include God in our evangelism efforts through prayer, Jesus makes an interesting statement. "Go! I am sending you out like lambs among wolves" (v. 3). *Wow!* That is not a real motivator there, Jesus! Who wants to be sent out like a lamb among wolves? Maybe this is why many people also share that their barrier is fear. They are afraid to share their faith because they are a lamb amongst wolves. A couple of things stand out as we look at this verse through the eyes of process. One, there is, in fact, an enemy who does not want us to share the good news of Jesus. We are told he prowls around like a roaring lion, seeking to devour (1 Pet 5:8). Two, sharing about Jesus and his kingdom is serious spiritual business, and we should not take it lightly.

If you were to put a lamb and a wolf together in the same pen, and you were to let them go at it in battle, wisdom would be to put your money on the wolf to win. I would put my money on the wolf every time to win—every single time except for one! That would be when the lamb is in the presence of the shepherd. If the shepherd is present, the wolf will flee. I think we can read here Jesus saying, "Hey, it is dangerous out there, but don't worry; I am with you, I got your back." King David is an excellent example of this. Remember when he was going to go up against Goliath and King Saul said, "Hey, you are only a young shepherd boy," but David responded:

> [34] "Your servant has been keeping his father's sheep. When a lion or a bear came and carried off a sheep from the flock, [35] I went after it, struck it and rescued the sheep from its mouth. When it turned on me, I seized it by its hair, struck it and killed it. [36] Your servant has killed both the lion and the bear; this uncircumcised Philistine will be like one of them because he has defied the armies of the living God. (1 Sam 17:34–36)

A lion or a bear is a lot scarier than a wolf, and the shepherd's job is to protect his flock of lambs. David knew where his real protection came from. "The Lord who rescued me from the paw of the lion and the paw of the bear will rescue me from the hand of this Philistine" (v. 37).

In all of our evangelism efforts, we are to go with the Shepherd. In verse 2 of our story, Jesus sends the seventy-two followers, two by two, to every city and place that he was going. Jesus is not asking us to do this alone; he will be with us. To support this truth, we only need to look at Matthew's explanation of the Great Commission. He ends the instructions of making disciples, baptizing, and teaching with a promise: ". . . And surely I am with you always, to the very end of the age" (28:20). In Acts 1:8, we read of the Great Commission as being empowered by the Holy Spirit to be witnesses. The Holy Spirit will come upon us and be with us. It is proper to read this verse in line with verse 5, where it is described that we will be baptized, immersed with the presence of the Holy Spirit. And we can be comforted by the exhortation we read in the book of Hebrews that "God has said, 'Never will I leave you; never will I forsake you.' So we say with confidence, 'The Lord is my helper; I will not be afraid. What can mere mortals do to me?'" (Heb 13:5–6). Not only does an ambassador represent the kingdom that sent them; they also go with the authority of that kingdom. Not only will you have the Shepherd's protection, but you will also have the Shepherd's authority.

The Great Commission in the Gospel of Mark remembers the call to preach the gospel is accompanied by a promise of authority. Jesus said, "In my name they will drive out demons; they will speak in new tongues; they will pick up snakes with their hands; and when they drink deadly poison, it will not hurt them at all; they will place their hands on sick people, and they will get well (Mark 16:17–18). Don't miss the key words in this passage: Jesus said, "*In my name . . .*" We never do anything in our own name or in the name of our church or pastor. We go with the power and authority that comes with the name of Jesus! Before we even begin to talk to someone about the truth and love of Jesus Christ, we need to communicate with Jesus through prayer. After Jesus instructs the seventy-two, first, to pray and, second, to make sure they go with the Shepherd, Jesus then instructs them on how to engage people

SPEAK GOOD NEWS

with good news. Like conquering the Slide for Life, being a bridge builder, or bridging the gap between man and God, is a process.

To illustrate this point, I want to share the marriage story of my friends Jack and Jennifer. They have been married for over thirty years now, which is remarkable when you understand how they started. Jack was visiting a local church for the first time that some of his friends had recommended. Between the worship time and the preaching, the pastor encouraged people to greet each other before they sat down. Jack saw this beautiful woman, Jennifer, and made a beeline straight for her. They introduced themselves, and Jennifer invited Jack to sit next to her for the rest of the service. After church was completed, Jack and Jennifer sat and talked for a while, and as they began to leave, they saw the pastor at the church door. Jack told the pastor the story of how they met each other during the greeting time and how they sat by each other the rest of the service. They talked briefly and asked the pastor if he would marry them immediately. The pastor was surprised but granted them their request. Right then, before leaving the church, the pastor married them. And they have been happily married for over thirty years now.

Now, if you think that story is amazing and a little unbelievable, you would be right. It is unbelievable because it never happened. The reason it never happened is because that is not how weddings happen. There is a process a couple goes through in joining in a covenant relationship. There is a time of introduction and courtship. The couple gets to know each other's likes and dislikes. They get to a point where they realize they cannot live without each other. So, they decide to seal their relationship in a covenant marriage. I think we would all agree that this is the normal process that most couples go through.

Looking at many evangelism strategies, programs, and methods, you will see that most of them look more like the made-up story of Jack and Jennifer meeting at church. For some reason, we have been taught that if we say the right words in the right order, we can convince someone to agree to join into a covenant relationship with Jesus after just one conversation. After you say yes to

Jesus, you can learn more about him, his likes and dislikes, etc. In the next chapter, we will continue looking at Jesus' instructions to the seventy-two, as he shows them a process in speaking good news in bridging the gap between lost people and himself.

8

Not Knowing What to Say: Part 2

A few years ago, while leading a group of college students on a mission trip to the nation of Trinidad and Tobago, both of my daughters, one a sophomore in college and the other a senior in high school, joined me on the trip. They understood that this trip was an evangelism-focused trip. We would be walking the streets of the community, offering to pray for people with the hope of sharing the gospel with them. This did not intimidate them because they both believed they would hang out with me and I would do all the talking. When we arrived at the church, we began to split the group into teams of two or three, one American per group. I could feel my daughters' eyes staring at me as they were paired off into different groups. I assured them that they would do fine, and to go out and enjoy their outreach. While walking with their group, the local ladies my daughter Allie was with looked at her and said, "This is great! You are Pastor David's daughter. I am sure you are an expert at this; show us how to do it!" Truth be told, this was the first time Allie had been on a mission trip; while she has heard me teach on this subject many times, she was a novice at putting it into practice. The assignment was to go to each home and business down the street and find people that might need prayer.

They went to a few homes, and Allie's confidence grew. The ladies she was with always asked her to lead out. They found themselves outside a business, where the business owners lived, so they went in. Once in the business, they realized they were in a neighborhood bar. The owner asked, "Can I help you?" Allie politely shared that they were Christians, offering prayer for anyone in need. Right away, a man spoke up and said that he needed prayer. He shared about some physical problems with his heart, but his biggest need was his family. He shared that he, his wife, and his daughter were Hindu and believed in prayer. But he was upset at his wife and daughter because his wife was living with another man, and his daughter was calling that man "Daddy"! He was now getting very upset, retelling the story. After listening to the man's need, Allie, while offering prayer, acknowledged that he said he was Hindu, and she assured him that she would be praying to and in the name of Jesus. The man replied that he was OK with that since he recognized Jesus as one of the many gods he served. The three ladies prayed for physical healing as well as for reconciliation in his family. After they prayed, Allie asked the man a question. "How does it make you feel that your wife and daughter are showing affection to another man?" He answered quickly, "I am mad; it makes me jealous; I am very angry about it." Then Allie said, "A minute ago, you said you believed in and worshiped Jesus as one of your gods. How do you think Jesus feels that you give the same worship and love to other gods?" The man was quiet. Allie went on to share that only Jesus loved him enough to die for him. Not only did he die, but he rose from the grave to prove he had power over sin and death. She reminded him that Jesus said he was the only way, truth, and life, and nobody comes to the Father except through him. The man was speechless and did not know how to respond.

    The point in sharing the above story is to point out that Allie was not given a script of what to say if she came across an angry Hindu whose wife and daughter were living with another man. No, she understood that having the right posture and mindset was more important than having a program or model to follow. She understood that she was an ambassador for Christ, and as his ambassador, she would share what he asked her to share. Jesus did not

SPEAK GOOD NEWS

let her down but opened the door for her to share what he brought to her mind. Her mindset was that of a bridge builder, bridging the gap between this man and God. As we continue looking at Jesus' instructions to the seventy-two, take note of certain postures and mindsets that Jesus is trying to instill in his followers.

SPEAK PEACE

After instructing the seventy-two to pray first and to go with the Shepherd, Jesus informs them of the importance of this mission by telling them not to be distracted or let anything interrupt the efforts. He then tells them what to say: speak peace (Luke 10:5). On this outreach, Jesus sends the seventy-two into towns and to homes. When I am asked, "David, tell me what to say," my response comes straight from verse 5: "When you enter a house, first say, 'Peace to this house.'" I say, "Speak peace." When Jesus instructs the seventy-two what to say, he might have told them several things to begin the conversation with. Notice he does not tell them, "Tell those in the home how bad they are!" or "Tell them that they are dirty, rotten sinners." While these statements may be true, that is not what Jesus tells them to do. He says, "Speak peace to this house." The gospel we get to share is a message of peace. It is a peace treaty between God and man, signed in the blood of Jesus Christ. This makes sense when you have a correct understanding of sin. Remember, sin does not make you bad; it makes you dead.

> If we reduce the purpose of evangelism to behavior modification, then speaking peace will not make sense to you.

But when we understand that sin makes a person dead, and we are sharing where we have found life and where they can find it, it becomes a message of peace.

So you may be thinking, "How does a person speak peace?" As mentioned previously, I define evangelism as intentionally engaging others in spiritual conversations that can lead to sharing the gospel. Speaking peace to me then would include words of kindness to the person you are conversing with. Being civil, courteous, and considerate to those we are engaging shows that we respect them. We are not putting ourselves above them, as if to communicate that we are better than they are. The only difference between us and them is that we have found new life in Jesus Christ; as Jesus told Nicodemus, we are "born again." Our main purpose is to lead them to where we found life, which can only be found in Jesus Christ. Speaking peace would include invoking the Prince of Peace in our conversations.

A while back, I was asked to conduct evangelism training for a church in the San Francisco Bay area. The pastor of this church wanted to go out into the community and share the love of Jesus with everyone who lived near the church. After the training sessions, we immediately put the training into practice by going in pairs of two into the community. I was paired up with a young girl in her early twenties named Ann. Ann and I went to an apartment complex near the church. Our approach was simple. We would introduce ourselves by name and let them know that we were Christians and taking some time out of our day to pray for our neighbors, asking them if there was anything, in particular, we could pray with them about. This is evangelism! Intentionally engaging others in spiritual conversations (can we pray for you) can lead to sharing the gospel. Most people appreciated the offer of prayer, and some even had serious issues that we invited the Prince of Peace into.

We knocked on this one door toward the end of the apartment complex. The door was immediately opened by a woman who had a very intimidating disposition. She stood at well over six feet. With her arms crossed, she asked, "What do you want?" I introduced Ann and myself, and she introduced herself as Tonya. We let her know that we were Christians and we were offering prayer for her. As soon as I mentioned that, she barked back, "Oh, you Christians want to pray for me? You really want to pray for me?" This was not said with an inviting tone but more as a challenge. I said, "Yes, we would like to pray," and again, she interrupted and

SPEAK GOOD NEWS

sarcastically stated, " So you Christians want to pray for me, huh? At this point I was trying to determine if we had found a "person of peace," it did not seem so. I was ready to excuse ourselves and move on. Then she said, "Sure, you Christians can pray for me!" Again, all this is in a very sarcastic tone. I replied, "Well, that is great; how can we pray for you? Is there anything specific we can pray about?" And with a smirk on her face, she said, "Yes, you can pray for my girlfriend and me!" She said this with her arms crossed, rocking her body back and forth, almost as a dare. Like, "I dare you to pray for my girlfriend and me!"

My response was quick and covered in peace. I said, "Great, we would love to pray for you and your girlfriend; what would you like us to pray for?" Remember, Jesus' instruction is to speak peace to this home! Immediately her disposition changed. She unfolded her arms, she bent down to make eye contact with me, and said, "You mean to tell me, that you, Christians, will pray for my girlfriend and me?" I repeated, "Yes, what would you like us to pray for?" She said, "Peace; can you pray for peace? It has been a long time since we have had peace in our home, we have been fighting, and neither of us can find employment that causes a lot of stress; please pray for peace." She mentioned the word *peace* four times. So I prayed. "Lord Jesus, my new friend Tonya is asking for your presence in her home. She realizes that she needs peace. Jesus, you are the Prince of Peace; without you, there is no peace. Lord, your Word states that if we invite you in, you will come. Tonya is inviting you into her home. As you bring peace to her home, Lord, would you also give her and her friend favor with employers, so they can work and have the means to survive? I pray this in your precious name. Amen." As I ended my prayer, I looked at Tonya, who was now wiping tears from her eyes. I then engaged her in a conversation by telling her a fact. I said, "Tanya, do you know that God thinks you are amazing?" She replied back, "No, he doesn't. Look at me; my life is a mess, and I have had many Christians tell me how bad I am," and she went on telling me of her past experience with Christians and the church. I shared with her that I cannot speak to what others have told her, but I can tell her what God says about her. I told her that an amazing God created her for an amazing purpose. I then asked her if she was living that purpose. She replied, "*No!*" I said, "Well, you are like most people I meet; they are trying to live their life according to God's purpose but fall short. The reason is that the Bible says that we have an enemy, who came to steal, kill, and destroy that purpose. But here is the good news [speak good news]: Jesus came to give us life!" You see, I did not tell her how bad she was; I shared with her where to find life. I intentionally engaged her in a spiritual conversation that led to sharing the gospel. She then leaned into her doorway and motioned to her friend, "Hey, we need to go to this guy's church!" I told her I was from another state, but Ann would be happy if she joined her. They exchanged information, and I understand that Ann made arrangements to bring Tonya and her friend to church.

We have opportunities like this every day. All we have to do is open our eyes and look. Remember, Jesus said the harvest is ripe. Who can you speak peace to today? If no one comes to mind, pray. Ask God to open your eyes to the person he has appointed for you to speak to today.

PRIORITIZE RELATIONSHIPS

Jesus, while instructing the seventy-two on what to do on their outreach as they speak peace, emphasizes the importance of prioritizing the person you are speaking with or engaging. He says, "Stay there, eating and drinking whatever they give you, for the worker deserves his wages. Do not move around from house to house. [8] When you enter a town and are welcomed, eat what is offered to you" (Luke 10:7–8). In this passage, Jesus highlights the importance of relationships. As we speak peace, we should also get to know people and enjoy the hospitality they offer. Now, I have heard well-meaning Christians say that there is a danger in this. We should not get too close to people who are not Christians. They are proof-texting the warning in 1 Corinthians 15:33, "Do not be misled: Bad company corrupts good character." While we should always ensure that the world does not influence us, we need to be

SPEAK GOOD NEWS

careful not to be so heavenly minded that we have no earthly good. We prioritize relationships because Jesus prioritized relationships.

Reflecting on my salvation story, I appreciate this aspect of the process. While I remember what I call my "aha moment," when my friend Tracy asked me, "David, what are you going to do about your faith and the knowledge you now have about Jesus?," the fact is that my finding life in Jesus Christ started a long time before that. As I have mentioned, growing up in a religious home, talking about spiritual matters with others was not foreign to me. However, it was not just the conversations that spoke the truth to me, but it was the love and acceptance being lived out in the lives of my friends. Just looking back at my senior year of high school, if my Christian friends did not prioritize having a relationship with me, I do not know if I would be writing this book today. Not every conversation I had with my friends was of a spiritual nature. However, their actions most certainly were. My friend Mike included me in many aspects of his life. His family welcomed me in. I was not treated like some outsider who belonged to a questionable religion. No, I was just David, Mike's friend.

This is a principle that we have taught our children. Every one of them have had friendships that, at one time or another, led them to engage their friends in spiritual conversations. Our youngest son, Jack, during his sophomore year of high school, became friends with a young man we will call "D," who had just moved to town. Besides hanging out and doing school activities, Jack began to invite D to our church's youth group. Jack continued being a good influence in D's life throughout the school year. The highlight of their friendship was when Jack led D into having his own relationship with Jesus, and Jack even baptized D at the end of the school year.

During Jack's senior year of high school, he befriended a new student who had just moved to the community. Jack invested a lot of time sharing with his new friend "E" about his faith and purpose in life. After Church one Sunday, Julie and I invited Jack out to lunch. We were to meet at a local restaurant at 1:00 p.m. Jack had to pick up E and give him a ride home, but he would meet us at the restaurant. We arrived at 1:00 p.m., but I did not see Jack. We were seated and I told the waitress we were waiting on one more. I looked at my watch; it was now 1:15, but still no Jack. I texted him to find out where he was. There was no reply to the text. We went ahead and ordered our lunch, and now it was 1:30, and still no Jack, and no response to our text. Jack arrived at the restaurant at 1:45, and I, being a little frustrated, said, "Jack, we were to meet at 1:00 p.m.; where were you?" And before I allowed him to answer, I said, "I texted you; why didn't you respond? Jack then said, "As I was taking E home, we began to talk about Jesus. He had a lot of questions, and I just spent time with him, trying to answer. And Dad, before I left, E said he wanted to start following Jesus, so he and I prayed together as he began his new life in Christ!"

That was the most loving and spiritual thing Jack could have done for E at that time.

> Prioritizing relationships is being a bridge builder, because people don't care how much you know until they know how much you care.

If we look around, we, too, can see people that need to be loved. Whom do you know that you can relationally invest in? When prioritizing relationships, we communicate to people that they are accepted and accepted as someone worthy to be loved by God.

ADDRESS THE BROKENNESS

As Jesus continues telling the seventy-two how to engage people in spiritual conversations, he says in verse 9, "Heal the sick who are there . . ." Remember, in Luke 9, Jesus appointed the disciples to proclaim the kingdom of God and to heal the sick (v. 2). Then he appoints the seventy-two to do the same in chapter 10. We are called to bring a presence of healing to those we are engaging. Now, in my tradition, I believe in physical healing. As James 5:15 instructs, I believe a "prayer offered in faith will make the sick person well."

SPEAK GOOD NEWS

Whenever I am sick, I want to be prayed for. As we engage people in spiritual conversations, we need to remember that everyone has experienced brokenness. Besides physical ills, people we engage with are suffering in other areas. People are in need of emotional healing, financial healing, relational and spiritual healing, and the list can go on. While everyone is in need of eternal healing from death to life as they put their faith in Jesus Christ, there are other areas in which God would like us to minister to people. God wants to use us as instruments of healing.

This is one of the points of the parable of the Good Samaritan we read about later in Luke 10. Here, Jesus is pointing out what it means to love our neighbors as ourselves. He contrasts the actions of some religious leaders, the Priest and Levite, to those of an unnamed Samaritan who saw a need and took it upon himself to meet it. The story goes that a man was lying on the side of the road, left for dead after being beaten and robbed. Along comes a priest, a religious leader, who sees the man, immediately crosses the road, and ignores the need to bring aid. Then a Levite, another religious person, walks by, sees the man, and goes on with his day, ignoring the opportunity to bring healing. Now, Jesus makes the point that both of these men acknowledged that a man needed help but consciously decided to leave him. Maybe they thought the man brought this upon himself and put himself in this situation, so he deserved what he received. What excuses do we let run through our heads as to why we may not help someone in need? It may cost us time, energy, and resources. I guarantee you it will. But that is how we serve God on earth; by serving people.

The story goes on as a stranger, a Samaritan man, comes along, sees the man in need, and immediately jumps into action. He bandages the man's injuries using his own supplies, puts him on his donkey, and gets him to a place of shelter where the man can recover. The Samaritan even pays for the room and promises to return and pay more if needed. The Samaritan man does not care why the person was in the situation he was in. All he cares about is bringing healing to a hurting person. Jesus is sending out the seventy-two and us to preach the kingdom and to heal those in need. While this book is about one aspect of the mission of God, evangelism, or gospel proclamation, the act of healing goes hand in hand. Theologian John Stott argues that "Evangelism and compassionate service belong together in the mission of God."[1]

One of the deepest hurts I experienced was when my mother and father disowned me after I shared with them that I no longer wanted to be a Jehovah's Witness. After hearing this, I drove out to my friend Tracy's family home to share with them what had just happened. Tracy and her family always showed me kindness and accepted me for who I was. I had just been disfellowshipped from the Jehovah's Witnesses, which meant I was to have no relationship with any Jehovah's Witness, including my family. My parents informed me that I was no longer their son, and until I returned to the Jehovah's Witness faith, I should consider myself dead to them. Obviously, this was devastating to me. Tracy's entire family was welcoming and even offered me a place to stay for the evening. One of my fondest memories is of Tracy's mother, Kris. While most of the family went to bed that night, I remember Kris staying up to talk with me. She was not preaching to me; she was just talking. She asked what I wanted to do with my life and if I thought about going to college or a trade school. While I do not remember everything we talked about—it seemed to last for hours—I do remember Kris addressing my brokenness, bringing healing to my hurt. Kris was simply a mom. She was talking to a young man who, in essence, had lost his parents. She was being a mom!

If you want to find someone ripe to share the gospel with, find someone who needs healing. Do your best to meet that need. It may come down to the fact that the only answer is God intervening in their circumstance, so you pray to the Great Physician to bring healing and restoration to their situation. It could be as simple as giving a seventeen-year-old boy a place to sleep for the night because his family has just disowned him. Or it could be purchasing some groceries for a family in need or paying their electric bill. There is a saying that people don't care how much we know until they know how much we care. James said it this way:

---

1. Stott, *Christian Mission*, 27.

SPEAK GOOD NEWS

"If one of you says to them, 'Go in peace; keep warm and well fed,' but does nothing about their physical needs, what good is it? . . . Show me your faith without deeds, and I will show you my faith by my deeds" (Jas 2:16, 18).

TELL THEM ABOUT THE KINGDOM

Jesus is training the seventy-two to go out and speak good news to the brokenhearted. He does so by telling them first to speak peace, then to prioritize relationships, followed by healing the sick or addressing the brokenness in the world. We should remember that Jesus describes the proper mindset and posture when engaging others in spiritual conversations. Christians should be the kindest, most generous people on earth. In verse 9, Jesus continues his instructions by saying, "Heal the sick who are there and *tell* them, 'The kingdom of God has come near to you.'" Tell them, communicate with words, that the kingdom of God is near. This is a vital part of evangelism. We could speak peace, prioritize relationships, and even serve people in meeting felt needs, and we can still fall short of communicating to them why we are doing it. In our society, there are many great service organizations that foster peace in the community, bring people together in relationships, and even serve people by bringing healing to felt needs. However, only the church of Jesus Christ has been given the stewardship of the gospel of Jesus Christ. It is our joy to tell people that the kingdom of God is close to them.

Remember, in chapter 2, I discussed the need to redeem evangelism. I mentioned that the use of the word *euangalion* (gospel) was common in pre-Jesus times. Caesar Augustus had his *euangalion*, his proclamation that was issued to his kingdom. Essentially, he was communicating that there was a new king on the throne, and he should be seen as God and the world's savior. When we tell people that the kingdom of God has come near to them, we communicate that the King is near. Wherever the King is, so is his kingdom. The gospel (*euangalion*) of Jesus Christ states that a new King is on the throne. Jesus Christ is the Savior of the world. Like the Samaritan woman at the well, we are simply saying, "Come see a man! He is my King! I believe he is the world's Savior; come check him out for yourself." We have the privilege of carrying the kingdom of God into the lives of those that God has a put in our lives.

In the final two chapters, I will share my thoughts on how to speak good news, and how to tell people about the kingdom. As I do, remember that it is not so much about having the perfect words or script to share. But, having the right posture of seeing people not as subjects of God's wrath but as objects of his love, and having the mindset that we are ambassadors and priests, we are only sharing what Jesus is telling us to share, as we build bridges from our friends, classmates, coworkers, and neighbors, to a God that truly loves them

9

Tell Your Story!

My first ministry position was that of an intern in the student ministries department at First Family Church in Whittier, California. The church was pastored by Ronald Prinzing, one of the most dynamic and anointed leaders I have ever served under. I am blessed to be counted among the many men and women who went into full-time vocational ministry under Pastor Prinzing's leadership. Others would include Pastor Benny Perez, a good friend and peer mentor who is an incredible pastor, preacher, and leader serving in Las Vegas, Nevada. Another is Pastor Kurt Johnston, who went on to write numerous books and is the next-gen pastor at Saddleback Church in Lake Forest, California. The list goes on and on.

The youth pastor, Kent Miller, was going to be going on vacation, and he asked me to fill in and preach to the entire youth group, junior high through college age, during the midweek service. I was very excited; this would be my first time preaching to a large group. I prepared for a few weeks leading up to the service. I prayed, and I think I even spent some time fasting, wanting God to use me like he used the other aforementioned leaders at the church. The night arrived, and we had a packed house. The worship service before I preached was amazing. Since Kent was gone, Kurt showed up to support me. Let me tell you, I preached my heart out! It was an amazing experience. I even remember what I preached about that night—evangelism (I have been told that my guitar only has one string). Students responded to the message with excitement by making commitments to go and share their faith on their campuses. After that night, I knew that it was my calling to pastor, teach, and equip the church as an evangelist.

Before heading home that night, Kurt was waiting for me. I felt really confident, and I asked Kurt what he thought of the message and how he thought I did. Kurt looked me in the eye and said, "David, that was the best, that was the most amazing; I mean, that was one of the most spot-on impressions of Benny Perez I have ever seen." I responded with a nervous laugh and said, "Yeah, a . . . what?" He repeated, "That was the best impression of Benny Perez I have ever seen." He went on to say, "David, God has uniquely called you. He called David Schaal! He is not asking you to be a cheap imitation of Benny Perez! Benny is doing a great job at being Benny! But he also called a David Schaal, and what I saw tonight was not the David Schaal I know." A few months ago, I reminded Kurt of that night almost thirty years ago, and he laughed and apologized. But I told him not to apologize because that was the most significant truth anyone had ever shared concerning my calling.

WE ALL HAVE A STORY

So many times in the kingdom of God, we feel that we need to copy other people in order to have any relevance. If we mimic what we see and hear, we can "fake it till we make it." Sure, we can learn from others and are encouraged to do so. But learning from and copying are two entirely different things. This is a common frustration that Christians have with evangelism scripts and programs. While interviewing a young Christian woman in the Midwest, she told me she did not share her faith because it did not work. I asked her what she meant when she said that it did not work, and she responded, "I memorized the script, I shared the Scriptures and stories just like I was taught, and nothing happened. The person

SPEAK GOOD NEWS

I shared with did not want to follow Jesus, so it did not work for me." As a reminder, I am not saying that using a script, program, or model is wrong. In the next chapter, I will highlight a couple I have found useful.

To speak the good news of Jesus Christ to a world that desperately needs to hear about his truth and love, we must be ourselves and tell our story. First Peter 3:15 says it like this: "But in your hearts revere Christ as Lord. Always be prepared to give an answer to everyone who asks you to give the reason for the hope that *you* have. But do this with gentleness and respect" (emphasis added). We have our own story and reason why Jesus is our hope. You will notice Peter did not say, "Always be prepared to say the perfect words in the perfect order . . ." We all have our own story. Our testimony is our story; how we met Jesus, and what he has done for us.

After being set free from Babylonian captivity, the psalmist David wrote a thanksgiving hymn giving God honor and praise. Psalm 107 is a song of thanksgiving that also contains instructions for all of us who have been set free by God.

> [1] Give thanks to the Lord, for he is good;
> his love endures forever.
> [2] Let the redeemed of the Lord tell their story—
> those he redeemed from the hand of the foe,
> [3] those he gathered from the lands,
> from east and west, from north and south
> (Ps 107:1–3)

If God has set us free, we should shout it from the rooftops! We should take this Old Testament song of praise and thanksgiving and apply it to our own story of how Jesus has redeemed us and set us free from the captivity of sin. The Message Bible paraphrase reads, "Oh, thank GOD—he's so good! His love never runs out. All of you set free by GOD; TELL the world! Tell how he freed you from oppression." Every Christian has a story of how God has set them free, and the world deserves to hear our stories.

In the introduction of this book and in chapter 3, I highlighted the important aspects of my story. I have also woven the thread of my story throughout every chapter. We can communicate our Jesus story in many ways as we engage those God has put in our lives. Here is the interesting thing about stories: people want to hear them! Think about it; people binge-watch television series and go to the movies, not to mention the countless number of social media posts, videos etc., all trying to hear a story. The number of written books has increased over the years; in 2022, over 2.2 billion books were sold, and it is estimated that in 2023 that number will rise by 2.53 percent, or total sales of over $78 billion. And 55.5 percent of those books are fiction books, stories.[1] In Appendix B, I share a simple tool on "How to Tell Your Story." This tool will help you develop your story in a short, concise manner. This tool then will be your blueprint, only to be built upon as you practice telling your story, building an easy onramp for you to engage people in spiritual conversations by telling your story.

BEYOND OUR SALVATION STORY

Evangelism or speaking good news is not relegated only to our salvation story. Jesus is doing wonderful things in our lives each day. When we brag about what Jesus is doing in our lives, it becomes a story that never ends. That is what is taking place in the preceding verses of Psalm 107. We read story after story of how God rescued people from their distress. Verses 4–9 tell the story of helpless, homeless, and hungry individuals lost on a journey. They cried out to God, and he rescued them from their troubles. Verses 10–16 is a story of people who were on the verge of death due to their decisions to rebel against the word of God. They, too, cried out to God, and he rescued them from death and despair. Verses 17–22 is a story about foolish people who, as a result of their choices, became sick to the point of being unable to eat. They were close to death, and they cried out to God, and he healed them. Verses 23–31 tell the story of men doing business on the sea. They saw God's hand in the wind and the waves. They became troubled, being tossed back

---

1. Simon & Schuster, "Nonfiction Book Sales Statistics."

SPEAK GOOD NEWS

and forth, and they cried out to God, and he rescued them. Verses 33–42 explain how God has turned desolate areas into fruitful areas and dry wells to overflowing. God has produced crops and has not let their number of cattle decrease. God is worthy of praise! "Let the one who is wise heed these things and ponder the loving deeds of the LORD" (v. 43). When we share about God's love and provision, we are speaking good news. This is evangelism!

It is common for us to share stories with those we do life with. If my favorite sports team is victorious over the weekend, I guarantee you I will tell as many people as possible on Monday morning. I constantly share stories about my children and grandchildren with whoever will listen. I will let people know if Julie and I have found a new restaurant that we really like. The same may be true if we try a restaurant we do not like. We share stories about our life. To think evangelism is only telling people your salvation story would reduce this wonderful discipline to one aspect of speaking good news.

That would be like me telling people about Julie and only sharing the story of how she and I met and how we fell in love, and then how on October 6, 1990, we stood in front of a church packed with our family and friends and we both said, "I do"! That is only the beginning story. While I agree, the most important part of our story is not the whole or the end. I have books of stories about Julie that I can tell. How great of a mother and grandmother she is. How she keeps me centered in my calling as a husband, father, pastor, and evangelist. This book would not have been written without her constant encouragement and counsel. I can tell you stories of how great of a minister she is in her own right. How intelligent and educated she is. How wisdom spills over as she speaks. I can tell you how she is my most faithful advocate to the throne of God in her prayers. Oh, and her beauty! I can write volumes on that subject. Here is the point: I can share any of the above topics with you that will spark your interest to learn more.

> I intentionally engaged you in a conversation about Julie, which led to you wanting to meet her yourself.

Reasons We Don't Tell Our Story

As I have shared in previous chapters, the reasons we do not engage others in spiritual conversations have a lot to do with a misguided understanding of the gospel. When we think we need to tell people how bad they are or don't feel we are a good representation of the gospel, and with the fear of being a hypocrite, we don't say anything at all. We must understand the gospel is a story of God's love for his creations and how, through his love, he sent his Son Jesus to earth to pay the ultimate price for our sins. The sin that separated us from having a relationship with God has been conquered, and forgiveness is available through Jesus. This is the best story ever! This is good news, the good news we get to share with others. I trust that reading about how to overcome those obstacles has inspired and empowered you to get out there and tell your story.

We share things that we find exciting or fascinating, and often, we cannot wait to tell others. On the other hand, things that we find no life in will seldom be shared. As a new Christian, I could not wait to tell as many people as possible about Jesus. As I mentioned earlier, my excitement to share Jesus with others was met by the remark, "Oh, you will grow out of it; you are in the honeymoon stage now." At the time, I did not know what the lady was talking about, and I am sure glad I did not grow out of it. Sadly, though, many Christians have. They have forgotten about the excitement they felt when they first met Jesus. In his book *Contagious*, author and professor Jonathan Berger shares insight as to why some things are shared either through talking with someone or on social media, while others items are not. Several insights were gleaned, but the strongest discovery was that articles that drove a sense of awe into readers were thirty times more likely to make the list of "most shared articles."[2] The bottom line is that we can't help but spread news that we find amazing.

Life happens, and before we know it, we stop talking about what Jesus has done in our life, not because we stop believing in him; we stop telling our story because we get busy and life goes on.

---

2. Berger, Jonah. *Contagious: Why Things Catch On*.

SPEAK GOOD NEWS

It could be because we continually succumb to the temptation of sin and listen to the lies of the enemy that wants to tell us that our Jesus experience was not real. There could be many reasons. If I stopped talking to my wife, Julie, and we only passed by each other now and then, if we did not do life together, she probably would not be my second favorite topic to talk about. Restoring the joy and excitement of our relationship with Jesus can start by simply praying the prayer that David prayed after being confronted with his sin. He prayed, "Create in me a pure heart, O God, and renew a steadfast spirit within me. [11] Do not cast me from your presence or take your Holy Spirit from me.[12] Restore to me the joy of your salvation and grant me a willing spirit, to sustain me" (Ps 51:10–12). Return to me the *joy* of my salvation. The news we get to share is the greatest news ever. When the religious leaders asked Peter and John, two of Jesus' disciples, to stop speaking about Jesus, they replied, "We are unable to stop speaking about what we have seen and heard" (Acts 4:20). Can you imagine how fast and how far the gospel of Jesus Christ would spread if every Christian had the same feeling?

Reasons We Should Tell Our Story

When you are living a new life in Jesus Christ, there are always opportunities for you to share your story with others. Back in 1998, Julie, our two daughters, and I were on vacation in California. We made a little road trip up to the coast of California and took time to visit my two sisters, Keri and Kathy. It had been around fourteen years since I had seen both of my sisters together. We met at our grandmother's home; it was the first time my sister Keri met Julie and my daughters. We had a wonderful time catching up with each other, and my sisters spoiled my daughters. Before leaving, Keri looked at me and said, "David, I and the rest of the family are unhappy that you are no longer a Jehovah's Witness. However, I sure love the way you have turned out. You are a different man! You used to be angry; you had a temper; you were not nice to be around. But seeing you now and how you have changed, I really like seeing that." At the time, Keri gave credit to Julie, my wife. I said, "No, it is Jesus." I then shared my story of how Jesus had brought me peace, purpose, and life and how I lived with hope and not fear. I also told her that I had a lot of junk in my life that I was still working through, but Jesus was working on those right alongside me. I was bragging about Jesus. People will see that there is something different about you once you begin to live your life for Jesus. Now, I am not saying you will be perfect; like I told Keri, I am still working on stuff—aren't we all?

I told Keri I was not the same person I used to be, but I was not yet where I needed to be. It is this journey we take when we walk alongside Jesus. We will never share our story if we wait until we are perfect. That is why I love the story we shared in earlier chapters of the Samaritan woman at the well. The end of that story shows the power, purpose, and importance of why we need to tell our story. If you remember, she runs back to her village and shares her story of how she'd met Jesus. She says, "Come see a man; he told me everything I ever did! Could this be the Messiah?" Sharing our story has the ability to convince people to put their faith in Jesus. John 4:39: "Many of the Samaritans from that town believed in him because of the woman's testimony, "He told me everything I ever did." They believed in Jesus because she shared her story! Notice she shared her story before making any changes in her life.

> She shared her story before being baptized or attending a church membership class. She told her story before being told to do so.

She shared her story before attending an evangelism training course. She, like Peter and John, was unable to stop speaking about what she had seen and heard

Telling our story helps people put their faith in Jesus. Also, telling our story enables others to experience Jesus in a way that they now have their stories to share. We read on in the story, "[40] So when the Samaritans came to him, they urged him to stay with them, and he stayed two days. [41] And because of his words many

SPEAK GOOD NEWS

more became believers. [42] They said to the woman, 'We no longer believe just because of what you said; now we have heard for ourselves, and we know that this man really is the Savior of the world'" (4:40–42). They now have their own story.

YOUR STORY

Remember, the stories we share about Jesus do not have to be limited to our salvation experience. When we engage people in spiritual conversations, we tell people stories of our experience with Jesus. The story could be how God provided a job for you to be able to support your family, or how God brought healing to someone who was sick that you were praying for. Spiritual conversations could include some of the pain you have gone through and how you experienced God's faithfulness even through the pain. We get to highlight God's faithfulness and presence as we experience the pain.

When we do share our salvation story, there are three main parts or questions to answer when telling your story. First, what was your life like before you met Jesus? Second, how did you come to meet Jesus? And third, how has your life been different after meeting Jesus? My story: My life was in chaos and confusion, practicing a religious life that brought no peace. My classmates in high school shared the love of Jesus Christ by word and deed, which made him irresistible. I now live with a peace that can only come from knowing how much Jesus loves me and that he, in fact, is my Savior. Obviously, that is a very condensed version of the events. But answering those questions will help you articulate your Jesus story to others.

You may be saying, "I don't have a story; I was raised in the church." So you think you do not have a story. Well, that is the farthest thing from the truth. Years ago, as I began preaching and sharing more in churches, I had the opportunity to share my story with many people and groups. One day, while driving home, Julie looked over at me and said, "Hey, you know what? I have a better story than you!" I remember laughing out loud and saying, "What?

What are you talking about?" She went on to say, "I hear you share your story all the time whenever you get a chance to speak, and I just feel that my Jesus story is just as good, if not better, than yours." I said, "C'mon, you were raised in church; what do you mean you have a better story?" She said, "I was born on Mother's Day, dedicated to the Lord on Father's Day; there has not been a day in my life that I did not know of the love of God. When I was five years old, I asked Jesus to be my Savior. That was only confirming what I had felt all of my young life. David, God has protected me from all the pain, heartache, abuse, and sin you have experienced." I stopped her and said, "You are right; you have a better story." Then she once again corrected me and said, "*No*, not a better story, just my story, the story I will share with our kids, so they can also put their faith in Jesus early in life."

Before we move on to the next chapter, where I will highlight some points to remember as you prepare to share your story, let's do a little exercise. Please take out a piece of paper, or open up a notes app on your phone, and let's practice writing your story. The first thing I want you to do is to think back on how your life was before you met Jesus. How old were you? What was your life like? Were you happy, sad, or confused? What was your family life like? What was the most dominating thing that would define your lifestyle back then? Go ahead and take some time to write that out.

Once you complete that, write a paragraph on how you met Jesus. Who was the person that told you about Jesus? Was it a person at all? Was it a gospel tract or a portion of Scripture? Was it someone on TV, or was it a stranger that recited the "Romans Road" or the "Four Spiritual Laws" or any other evangelism strategy or model? How many conversations or interactions did you have with the person or device that introduced Jesus to you? Was it one conversation, ten, or one hundred? What created that aha moment where you knew you had to say yes to Jesus? How did you tell Jesus that you accepted his free gift of salvation and that you wanted to make him the leader, Lord of your life? Was it a prayer? Did someone lead you in prayer, or was it just you and Jesus?

SPEAK GOOD NEWS

Now, write out how your life has been since that day. Has your life been perfect, never making a mistake, never sinning again? Most likely not. I have never met anyone that could say yes to that question. Did you start going to church? Did your friends change? Even if you struggle in some areas, where have you found victory? Are you experiencing more peace in your life than you did before? Also, write out some of the spiritual goals that you made for yourself. These would be things in your life or a level of spirituality you want to achieve over the next six months. This could be something you would like to be more consistent in, lik reading the Bible. Or is it your prayer life that you would like to strengthen? Hopefully, after reading this book, you may have a goal of bragging about Jesus and speaking the good news of Jesus to more people than you have in the past.

You now have a blueprint of your story. Read this over and over. Once you do, you will notice a couple of things. With Jesus in your life, you are not the same as you once were. You may not be where you want to be, but you are not the same. Being honest about your story, your struggles, and making that a part of the story you share with people will ensure that you are being authentic and not hypocritical. I am not advising you to share everything you are struggling with. But allow the Holy Spirit to guide you. Showing some vulnerability will communicate to the person you are sharing with that you are honest and someone who can be trusted.

When sharing your story with others, I recommend you spend most of your time bragging about how Jesus is changing your life. Knowing where we have been is important, but knowing where we are and where we are going is of the utmost importance. Remember, your story is not a testimony of how the devil had influence and control over you; it is a story of how Jesus has redeemed you.

10

Ways to Speak Good News!

To get the full benefit of this chapter, I encourage you to finish the exercise at the end of chapter 9. We all have our unique story of how we encountered Jesus. Others may have a similar story, but yours is different. Just as your relationship with Jesus is distinctive and personal, so is your story. Nobody should be able to take that away. Faithful Christians have used many programs, methods, and scripts to share their faith with non-Christians over the years. As I have mentioned earlier, I have used many of these myself.

Unashamedly, this book aims to see faithful Christians living a life on mission where they speak the good news of Jesus Christ to their circle of influence as commonly as they share other positive stories. Can you imagine what would happen if the 85 percent of Christians who are currently allowing a barrier to keep them from engaging in spiritual conversations started bragging about their Bridegroom, Jesus? That would be incredible! With that, I want to mention that we, as Christ-followers, should have at least a rudimentary understanding of the important aspects of sharing the gospel. Sure, we need to start somewhere, and I encourage you to start telling people about your hope in Jesus Christ. One point of this chapter is to give the reader some understanding of key components of the gospel, not so much so that you would have to

SPEAK GOOD NEWS

repeat this verbatim, as much as have a knowledge of key topics. I will share my two favorite approaches to speaking good news in this chapter.

In the autumn of 2017, Every Home for Christ launched its ministry in the United States. As part of the leadership team, we began a season of research and development. Some of those results I have already shared in this book. On one occasion, we invited over sixty leaders from around the country who either ran or served in an evangelism-focused ministry. We had a variety of ages and cultural backgrounds, males and females from across the United States. The purpose of this gathering was to learn from leaders, to see what they were doing in their area of responsibility, and then share with them what we at Every Home USA were learning from our research.

During this meeting, we asked the leaders to have a discussion around their tables and share with each other their "come to Jesus" story. We asked that each person take the time needed to share their story and then listen to the different ways that people met Jesus. This proved to be a valuable exercise. Everyone shared around the table I was sitting at, and as interesting as each story was, there were no duplicates. After everyone had a chance to share their story around the table, we asked for one person from each table to share with the entire group. It was interesting to hear the many ways that Jesus met people and how they met Jesus. While no story was identical, they all had some noteworthy commonalities. None of these leaders came to Christ after hearing a perfectly recited script. None put their faith in Jesus after the initial conversation or contact with the Christian sharing with them—the majority shared about multiple conversations lasting many months and even years. While some did share about the need to deal with their sinful lifestyle, it was not their lifestyle that provoked them to say yes to Jesus. Being confronted about their lifestyle was not the first time they realized something was wrong. A void needed to be filled, and their lifestyle choices were just means of trying to fill it. The overwhelming deciding factor for each of these leaders was coming to grips with how much God loves and accepts them. If

WAYS TO SPEAK GOOD NEWS!

you completed the exercise at the end of chapter 9, I am sure your story is similar to those mentioned above.

We then asked the group of evangelism leaders to answer this question around their tables: "What would you say if you were to engage non-Christians in a conversation with the hope of sharing the gospel with them?" Or, "How would you lead someone to Christ?" Now, before your read on, answer that question yourself. Given the opportunity, how would you lead someone to Christ? Please take a moment and write it out like the previous exercise.

The conversation around the tables started to become animated. Each leader was excited to share his or her preferred method of leading someone to Christ. One by one, the leaders shared a program, method, and script that they felt was the most effective way to lead someone to Christ. How about you? Did you write down a popular method or program? As we went around the room, we realized that the methodologies shared differed from what the leaders shared earlier of how they came to Christ. While being somewhat an unscientific pole, we could conclude that very few people come to Christ after just one conversation with a stranger who recited a perfectly worded script.

> If this is an accurate assumption, why do we continue teaching evangelism as a marketing plan for the church?

Why do we teach people to "close the deal" and move on to the next customer?

Once Every Home USA's leadership team realized this gap, we prayed to the Lord and searched the Scriptures to develop what we felt would be Evangelism or Gospel 101, meaning, what could a Christian share with a non-Christian that, after the conversations, it would feel like the gospel was spoken and shared? What seeds were planted, nurtured, and possibly even harvested? We focused our attention on the Gospel of John.

SPEAK GOOD NEWS

THE GOOD NEWS ACCORDING TO JOHN

> The gospel is the good news that God showed his *love* for us by sending his Son to earth in the person of Jesus Christ, to live a sinless life that we could not, and die the death we should in our place. Three days later, he came back to life, proving he is the Son of God, providing forgiveness of sins and the gift of *life* and salvation to anyone who would *look* to him and believe in him alone. He provides the Holy Spirit to *lead* us as we live on earth, helping us live the life we were created to live.

Love

The gospel is good news! The story of humankind starts with a loving God's passion and love for his creation. We were created to have a life-giving, purposeful relationship with our creator, God! God loves us so much! Humankind is not the subject of God's wrath; we are objects of his love! Hearing that we are loved is good news. So many people think God is mad at us, waiting for us to mess up so he can discipline us. But we read of a different God in Scripture.

> [16] For God so loved the world that he gave his one and only Son, that whoever believes in him shall not perish but have eternal life. [17] For God did not send his Son into the world to condemn the world, but to save the world through him. (John 3:16–17)

This is probably the most popular passage in the Bible. It speaks of God's love and how he is offering life to all who believe. When we share how much God loves them, we share the good news, which is the gospel. When we read the narrative of Jesus in the Bible, we see the story of a man on a mission. This mission became necessary the moment Adam fell, because Adam's sin brought immediate separation from God and his creation. Genesis 3:15 says, "I will put enmity between you and the woman, and between your offspring and her offspring, he shall bruise your head, and you shall bruise his heel." Think about this: the moment God confronted Adam and Eve about their sin of eating fruit from the forbidden tree—not a year, a month, or a week later, not even one hour later, but right at the moment—God shared his plan to make things better, to restore what was stolen, to repair what was torn apart. Such an immediate response was made out of a posture of love. And the gospel, the good news of Jesus Christ, is bathed in the love of God, *agape* love. Sharing with people who do not have a relationship with Jesus that God loves them is good news. This is evangelism.

Life

Remember, sin does not make us bad; it makes us dead. So, the obvious answer to why Jesus had to come to earth was to pay the penalty of our sin, death, by giving his life as the final payment. When Jesus gave his life on the cross, he cried, *Tetelestai*, "It is finished!" (John 19:30). A better translation for *tetelestai*, with the verb *teleō*, would be, "It is accomplished" or "It is paid in full"! This is why, during his earthly ministry, he could proclaim confidently.

> The thief comes only to steal and kill and destroy; I have come that they may have life, and have it to the full. (John 10:10)

In man's pursuit to find hope and happiness, there are many other options out there, other faiths, and other leaders to follow. But Jesus calls all these thieves and robbers. All other ways lead to loss, death, and destruction. Jesus alone gives life and brings restoration—beginning with the life cut short in the garden of Eden. Not only does he offer life, but the quality of that life is also described as "to the full"!

The penalty for all of our sins has been paid. Yes, sin causes death, but Jesus conquered the last enemy, death (1 Cor 15:26). He reversed the curse of death handed down in the garden of Eden. Not only do we live with the hope of life everlasting, but the quality of our life in the here and now improves. It improves because we now live confidently that God is for us, not against us. This is good news!

SPEAK GOOD NEWS
Look

If God loves us by sending his Son Jesus to earth, and Jesus offers us life through his death and resurrection, how do we obtain it? This is a great question, and it is similar to what Jesus' Jewish audience was asking him in John 6. They asked, "Rabbi, what does the Father require of us?" I could imagine they wondered if it was obeying the Ten Commandments or obeying all 613 Jewish laws. They were like, "Give us the bottom line, what do we need to do?" Jesus said, "to believe in the one he has sent" (vv. 28–29) Then later, he says,

> "For my Father's will is that everyone who looks to the Son and believes in him shall have eternal life, and I will raise them up at the last day." (John 6:40)

The word translated "look" in biblical Greek is *theōrō* (*tho-though*). It is defined as "experience in the sense of partaking of something."[1] To experience death—"Those that obey my words will not look upon death" *(*John 8:51). Jesus is not saying all we have to do is glance at him; no, he is saying that we need to experience him enough that we begin to put our trust in him. The word translated "believe" is the same word used earlier in John 3:16, *pisteúsō*. It is more than just some intellectual thought; it is deeper; it means to put our trust in him. In the Gospel of John, this word is used eighty-four times.

- To Martha at Lazarus' tomb: "'Everyone who lives and believes in me shall never die. Do you believe this?' She said to him, 'Yes, Lord; I believe that you are the Christ, the Son of God, who is coming into the world.'" (11:26–27)

- To Thomas: "Then he said to Thomas, 'Put your finger here, and see my hands; and put out your hand, and place it in my side. Do not disbelieve, but believe.' Thomas answered him, 'My Lord and my God!' Jesus said to him, 'Have you

---

1. Zodhiates, *Complete Word Study Dictionary*.

believed because you have seen me? Blessed are those who have not seen and yet have believed.'" (20:27-29)

Humankind is to look to the Son, the one God has sent, and believe, trust, in him for salvation. Those that do, Scripture says, will have eternal life. This means trusting wholeheartedly in Jesus alone for eternal life. This is good news!

Lead

Now that we understand God's love for us, and that Jesus gave his life so we can now have life by the debt of our sin being paid in full by him, and that we receive that by putting our trust in Jesus alone, what is next? Here is a beautiful reminder to those that allow the barrier of not wanting to be pushy or confrontational, or think they have to call someone out on their sin, to stop them from speaking good news. I hope this passage sets you free.

> [8] When he comes, he will prove the world to be in the wrong about sin and righteousness and judgment: . . . [13] But when he, the Spirit of truth, comes, he will guide you into all the truth. He will not speak on his own; he will speak only what he hears, and he will tell you what is yet to come. [14] He will glorify me because it is from me that he will receive what he will make known to you. (John 16:8, 13-14)

First off, in this passage, Jesus is introducing the Holy Spirit and His job to bring conviction to people about sin, righteousness, and judgment. It is not your job! Now, the Holy Spirit may use you to share with others about sin, righteousness, and judgment, but it is solely in his job description to bring conviction. God has given us the Holy Spirit to lead our lives. We need to follow the leading of the Holy Spirit. I have been serving Jesus now for over four decades. The Holy Spirit is still guiding and directing my steps. He also convicts me when I stray from the path he is leading me on. Let me tell you, this is good news that God would love us so much that he would send his Son Jesus to pay the price of our sins and

SPEAK GOOD NEWS

offer us life through experiencing, believing, and trusting in him. We also now have the Holy Spirit guiding and leading our lives. This is the gospel; this is good news!

Now, I look at these four L words I have just discussed as pillars or foundational posts in speaking good news. Some would suggest that the lack of talking about the cross or sin would seem to be sharing an incomplete gospel. I am not suggesting that we never discuss the cross, sin, the resurrection, or turning from our sinful lifestyles. I suggest we do not have to tell a non-Christian everything we know about the Bible in our initial conversations with them. It is a process. As you have continued conversations with people, you can go deeper as the conversation directs.

I have shared the "Good News According to John" with many Christians who would consider themselves a part of the 85 percent who want to share their faith but allow a barrier to keep them from doing so. The most common response is, "I can do that!" We see faithful Christians across the U.S. willing to tell people of God's love as they engage people in spiritual conversations that lead them to share the gospel.

THE GO5PEL IN FIVE WORDS

Shortly after putting the "Good News According to John" on paper, I wanted to share it with some of my friends and mentors. One of those was Kurt Johnston, the next-gen pastor at Saddleback Church in Lake Forest, California. I went through each step with Kurt, and we had a wonderful discussion about seeing faithful Christians actively share the love of Jesus with a world that so desperately needs to know Jesus. Kurt mentioned that just a few years earlier, he also put together some teachings on how to share the gospel.

Kurt wanted to ensure they each year, when they had a new crop of student leaders, at the minimum, they would understand how to share the gospel with students who had questions. Kurt and his team created "The Go5pel in Five Words." I have found this to be a very easy and accurate way to talk to people about the love of

WAYS TO SPEAK GOOD NEWS!

Jesus. I have shared this in one-on-one conversations, at funerals, and even on the foreign mission field. Each time I share these five words, I sense the Holy Spirit using them to move non-Christians a little closer to God.

> *God* created all of us with the intention of being in a perfect relationship with him that would last forever. Sadly, that relationship was broken when people chose to *sin* and follow their ways instead of God's. To fix the broken relationship, God sent his only Son, *Jesus Christ*, to die on the cross and pay the penalty for our sins. Jesus' death and resurrection paved the way to a restored relationship with God and a forever life in heaven, which he offers us a free *gift*! God loves us completely and will never force us to follow him, so he gives us the *choice* to receive or reject this amazing gift!

God

The very first words in the Bible are, "In the beginning, God . . ."! The entire story of the all-encompassing universe is about God. It is his story, a love story. Our very existence is connected to God!

> An amazing God has created us for an amazing purpose. The purpose is to have an everlasting relationship with him, and to be fruitful and multiply, to have dominion over the earth. We were created for God's pleasure.

> [26] Then God said, "Let us make man in our image, in our likeness, so that they may rule over the fish in the sea and the birds in the sky, over the livestock and all the wild animals, and over all the creatures that move along the ground." [27] So God created mankind in his own image, in the image of God he created them; male and female he created them. (Gen 1:26–27)

SPEAK GOOD NEWS

Out of all of creation, only humans were created in the likeness of God (Gen 5:1). The purpose and plan for our lives was put in jeopardy when the first created people, Adam and Eve, chose to disobey God. The Bible calls this "sin"; every human has inherited a sinful nature.

Sin

God told his beloved creation that they could eat from any tree in the garden except for one, the tree of the knowledge of good and evil. God told them that if they ate of the tree, they will surely die (Gen 3:17). They chose to eat. This did not make them bad; it made them dead. The penalty for their choosing to sin was death in their relationship with God. The relationship between God and his creation was now broken. This is why the world is full of broken people, because our relationship with God is broken. According to the Bible, we all have sinned and are separated from God, which results in death.

> Therefore, just as sin entered the world through one man, and death through sin, and in this way death came to all people, because all sinned. (Rom 5:12)

When people choose to sin, they choose their way instead of God's. This results in brokenness and death. But all is not lost! To fix the broken relationship problem, God sent his Son, Jesus!

Jesus Christ

In the exact same chapter of the Bible (Genesis 3) that we read of God's creation choosing to sin against God, we also read of God's plan to restore the relationship. In verse 15, we read of God's plan for redemption. Romans 6:23 tells us the magnitude of sin, and how Jesus takes care of the sin problem: "For the wages of sin is death, but the gift of God is eternal life in Christ Jesus our Lord." The penalty of sin is death, but Jesus is offering us eternal life! Because of God's love for us, he sent his one and only Son,

Jesus, to die on the cross and then rise from the grave to pay the penalty of our sins and fix what has been broken. Jesus' death and resurrection pave the way to a restored relationship with God and reverse the curse of death by offering everlasting life with him in heaven. Here is the astonishing part: he offers all of this as a free, no-strings-attached gift!

Gift

The life that Jesus is offering is a free gift (Rom 6:23). If we had to pay for it ourselves or do some labor to receive it, it would no longer be considered a gift. I am sure you have received and given gifts in the past. When we give a gift to a person, we do not expect any payment in return. Salvation, this life that Jesus is offering, he is offering as a free gift.

> For it is by grace you have been saved, through faith—and this is not from yourselves, it is the gift of God—not by works, so that no one can boast. (Eph 2:8–9)

By putting our faith in what Jesus did for us on the cross, we now have the ability to be in the right standing with God, to have that relationship that was cut off in the garden of Eden restored. We have now been justified by the grace of Jesus Christ (Rom 3:21–26). Even though God loves us completely, he will never force us to choose him; he gives us all a choice.

Choice

We have the choice to receive or reject this amazing gift. Here's the deal! The free gift of forgiveness of our sins, salvation, and eternal life is offered to everyone, but each person must make a choice to accept and receive this gift themselves.

> If you declare with your mouth, "Jesus is Lord," and believe in your heart that God raised him from the dead, you will be saved. For it is with your heart that you

SPEAK GOOD NEWS

> believe and are justified, and it is with your mouth that you profess your faith and are saved. (Rom 10:9–10)

When you hear the good news about what Jesus did for you and what he offers you, it's up to you whether you believe or reject it. No one else can make this choice for you. It's a decision you have to make for yourself. The Bible makes it very clear what it means once you make the choice to receive this gift. "Yet to all who did receive him, to those who believed in his name, he gave the right to become children of God—children born not of natural descent, nor of human decision or a husband's will, but born of God" (John 1:12–13). When we choose the gift of salvation that Jesus offers, we become born again; born of God; we have a new life, eternal life.

MAKING A PLAN

Evangelism is simply communicating the good news of Jesus Christ to others. It is like a bride bragging about her bridegroom.

> It is not telling people how bad they are, but telling people where to find life.

It is also not trying to be someone you are not, but being honest with yourself and others, that we are all a work in progress. It is not trying to close the deal by convincing someone to say a special prayer as a salesman would. Evangelism is a process. Seeds are planted, watered, and nurtured, and when God sees the timing is right, he brings the increase or person to the point of decision. We disciple people as we tell them the beauty of the things of God. This happens before salvation (discipleship in utero)and does not stop when someone becomes born again. Speaking peace, prioritizing relationships, addressing the brokenness, and telling people that the kingdom of God has come near are all part of the process. The reason the kingdom has come near is because the King is near. When we evangelize and speak good news, we are communicating to people, "There is a new King ruling my life; his name is Jesus, and he is the Savior of the world."

WAYS TO SPEAK GOOD NEWS!

There is a saying that goes, "If you fail to plan, you are planning to fail!" Good intentions are not worth anything if there is no follow-through. As I have traveled the USA and spoken with hundreds of faithful Christians, the majority would admit to having intentions of sharing their faith and their Jesus story with others, only to fall short and not say anything at all. Many of them would admit to allowing a barrier to keep them from having spiritual conversations. Hopefully, now that you are at the end of this book, you have been emboldened to go out there and speak the good news of Jesus Christ to people you know who do not know Jesus yet.

As a final exercise, let's make a plan to put what you have learned into action. The first thing I would like you to do is make a list of five to ten people in your life that you would like to see find new life in Jesus Christ. These can be family members, coworkers, classmates, neighbors, etc. Once you have completed this list, begin praying for each one by name. Every day, lift up the list, one by one, by name, asking God to open a door for you to engage them in a spiritual conversation. As you pray, look for those open doors you are praying to be opened. Once the door is open, open your mouth, and *speak good news*!

Appendix A

Mission Flowchart

The chart below shows the progression of the mission of God, with its origin rooted in God himself. God's mission has a church, and the church has two distinct roles to perform: first, to participate and fulfill the Great Commandment of loving God and loving our neighbors; second, this should naturally flow into participation in the Great Commission, our common mission of making disciples by teaching and training, which leads to proclaiming and telling others about the love of Jesus. This book is focused on the evangelism aspect (highlighted with the border) of the Great Commission. As you can see, conviction and conversion are left up to God the Holy Spirit (John 16:7–1).

APPENDIX A

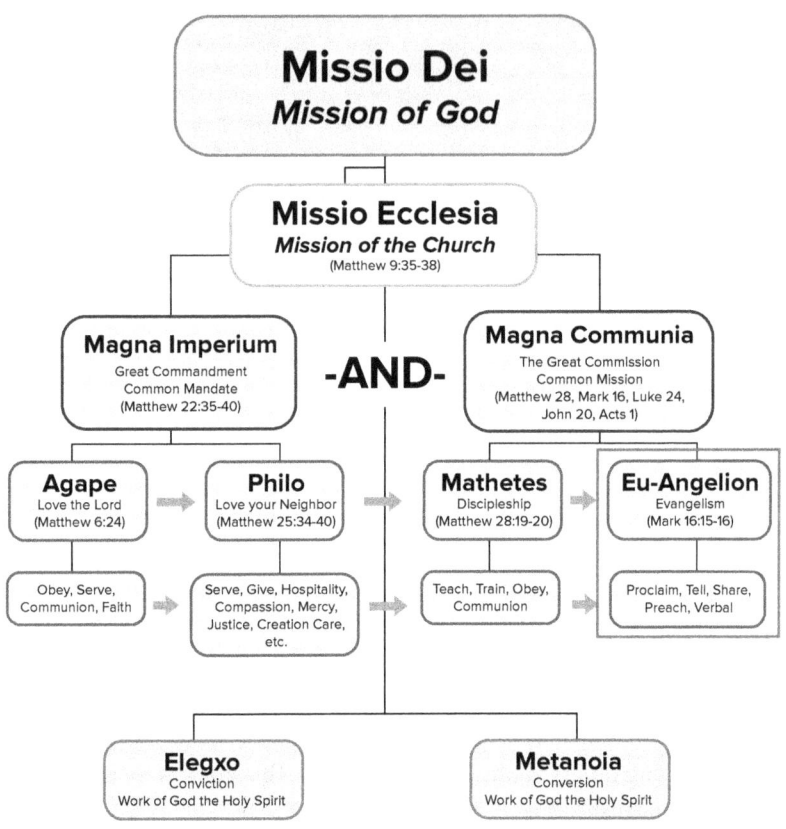

Mission Flowchart (© Speak Good News)

Appendix B

How to Tell Your Story

Let the redeemed of the Lord tell their story (Ps 107:2)

Every one of us has a unique story of how we came to know and put our trust in Jesus Christ. While we are indebted to the person who introduced us to Jesus, we carry a duty to share our story of faith with as many individuals as possible. Psalm 107 serves as a guide for shaping our personal stories, aiming to captivate the curiosity of those we share with and ignite in them a desire to know more about Jesus, our Lord.

In retelling our story, we could focus on four distinct areas found in each of the stories in Psalm 107:

- our life prior to embracing Jesus
- the journey leading us to know Jesus
- our transformed life after embracing Jesus
- telling of the greatness of Jesus

APPENDIX B

OUR LIFE PRIOR TO EMBRACING JESUS

Think back to the time before you were introduced to Jesus. Make a list of the things you used to do or the way you used to think. Maybe you were raised in a non-Christian religion. Or perhaps you knew nothing about God or his plan for your life. Highlight the emptiness and loneliness of living life with no guidance or direction.

THE JOURNEY LEADING US TO KNOW JESUS

When and how were you introduced to Jesus? Was it a crisis? Was it a classmate sharing with you over a period of time? Was there a particular Bible passage or prayer that convinced you to put your faith in Jesus? Think back to that "Aha" moment when you said yes to Jesus, crying out to him to be your Lord and Savior.

OUR TRANSFORMED LIFE AFTER EMBRACING JESUS

How has your life changed after you said yes to Jesus? Highlight and contrast the changes from your life prior to embracing Jesus. Do you have more peace in your life? Do you now live with the confidence that you are truly loved and accepted by God? How do you see God working in your life today?

TELLING OF THE GREATNESS OF JESUS

Looking over the first three steps, how would you now share with others what Jesus has done in your life? Make a list of the areas in your life where Jesus has transformed you. Write out a sentence or two, or make a bulleted list of items, to brag to others about what Jesus has done in your life.

HOW TO TELL YOUR STORY

EXAMPLES OF THOSE STORIES FOUND IN PSALM 107

Prior to Embracing Jesus	*Leading Us to Know Jesus*

⁴Some wandered in desert wastelands,
    finding no way to a city where they could settle.
⁵ They were hungry and thirsty,
    and their lives ebbed away
	⁶Then they cried out to the Lord in their trouble,
	    and he delivered them from their distress.

Life after Embracing Jesus	*Telling of the Greatness of Jesus*

⁷He led them by a straight way
    to a city where they could settle.
	⁸Let them give thanks to the Lord for his unfailing love
	    and his wonderful deeds for mankind,
	⁹ for he satisfies the thirsty
	    and fills the hungry with good things

Prior to Embracing Jesus	*Leading Us to Know Jesus*

¹⁰Some sat in darkness, in utter darkness,
    prisoners suffering in iron chains,
¹¹ because they rebelled against God's commands
    and despised the plans of the Most High.
¹² So he subjected them to bitter labor;
    they stumbled, and there was no one to help.
	¹³Then they cried to the LORD in their trouble,
	    and he saved them from their distress.

Life after Embracing Jesus	*Telling of the Greatness of Jesus*

¹⁴He brought them out of darkness, the utter darkness,
    and broke away their chains.
	¹⁴Let them give thanks to the LORD for his unfailing love
	    and his wonderful deeds for mankind,
	¹⁶ for he breaks down gates of bronze
	    and cuts through bars of iron.

APPENDIX B

HERE IS HOW THE APOSTLE PAUL TOLD HIS STORY TO KING AGRIPPA IN ACTS 26 USING THIS METHOD

Prior to Embracing Jesus	*Leading Us to Know Jesus*
[9] "I too was convinced that I ought to do all that was possible to oppose the name of Jesus of Nazareth. [10] And that is just what I did in Jerusalem. On the authority of the chief priests I put many of the Lord's people in prison, and when they were put to death, I cast my vote against them. [11] Many a time I went from one synagogue to another to have them punished, and I tried to force them to blaspheme. I was so obsessed with persecuting them that I even hunted them down in foreign cities.	[12] "On one of these journeys I was going to Damascus with the authority and commission of the chief priests. 13 About noon, King Agrippa, as I was on the road, I saw a light from heaven, brighter than the sun, blazing around me and my companions. 14 We all fell to the ground, and I heard a voice saying to me in Aramaic,[a] 'Saul, Saul, why do you persecute me? It is hard for you to kick against the goads.'
Life after Embracing Jesus	*Telling of the Greatness of Jesus*
[15] "Then I asked, 'Who are you, Lord?' " 'I am Jesus, whom you are persecuting,' the Lord replied. [16] 'Now get up and stand on your feet. I have appeared to you to appoint you as a servant and as a witness of what you have seen and will see of me. [17] I will rescue you from your own people and from the Gentiles. I am sending you to them [18] to open their eyes and turn them from darkness to light, and from the power of Satan to God, so that they may receive forgiveness of sins and a place among those who are sanctified by faith in me.'	[19] "So then, King Agrippa, I was not disobedient to the vision from heaven. [20] First to those in Damascus, then to those in Jerusalem and in all Judea, and then to the Gentiles, I preached that they should repent and turn to God and demonstrate their repentance by their deeds. [21] That is why some Jews seized me in the temple courts and tried to kill me. [22] But God has helped me to this very day; so I stand here and testify to small and great alike. I am saying nothing beyond what the prophets and Moses said would happen— [23] that the Messiah would suffer and, as the first to rise from the dead, would bring the message of light to his own people and to the Gentiles."

HERE IS MY STORY. . . .

Prior to Embracing Jesus	*Leading Us to Know Jesus*
I was raised in a religious home that did not see Jesus as Lord. I lived a life empty of any peace or purpose. I lived my life thinking I had to earn God's love and earn my salvation. I always came up short, which made me feel further from God.	My classmates in high school intentionally engaged me in spiritual conversations during my senior year of high school. I would listen to their stories of faith and wonder why I was not experiencing the same thing in my own life. They would live their life with peace and joy. They had a confidence that God loved them, which was evident by the way they lived their lives. I came to the point of desiring that same life and peace, which led me to say yes to Jesus.
Life after Embracing Jesus	*Telling of the Greatness of Jesus*
My life changed the day I said yes to Jesus! It was as if a weight had been lifted from my shoulders. No longer was I living my life to earn God's love; I was living my life knowing God loved and accepted me. I truly felt as if I went from death to life.	I have dedicated my life to telling as many people as possible about my story and where I have found life. I cannot not boast about my Jesus. I prayerfully ask the Lord to open up doors of opportunity, with the sole purpose of sharing my story about Jesus to others.

APPENDIX B

NOW, WRITE OUT YOUR STORY

Prior to Embracing Jesus	*Leading Us to Know Jesus*
Life after Embracing Jesus	*Telling of the Greatness of Jesus*

Tell Your Story Method (© Speak Good News)

Bibliography

Abraham, William J. *The Logic of Evangelism*. Grand Rapids: Eerdmans, 1989.

Barna, George. *Translating the Great Commission: What Spreading the Gospel Means to U.S. Christians in the 21st Century*. Ventura, CA: Barna Group, 2018.

Barrett, David B. *Evangelize!: A Historical Survey of the Concept*. Birmingham: New Hope,1987.

Berger, Jonah. *Contagious: Why Things Catch On*. Reprint. New York: Simon & Schuster, 2016.

Bosch, David Jacobus. *Transforming Mission: Paradigm Shifts in Theology of Mission*. Maryknoll, NY: Orbis, 1991.

Chan, Sam, and D. A. Carson. *Evangelism in a Skeptical World: How to Make the Unbelievable News about Jesus More Believable*. Grand Rapids: Zondervan Academic, 2018.

Church of England. *The Evangelistic Work of the Church: Being the Report of the Archbishop's Third Committee of Inquiry*. London: SPCK, Church of England, 1918.

Clinton, J. Robert. *Focused Lives: Inspirational Life Changing Lessons from Eight Effective Christian Leaders Who Finished Well*. Altadena, CA: Barnabas, 1995.

Covey, Stephen R. *The Seven Habits of Highly Effective People: Restoring the Character Ethic*. Boston: G.K. Hall, 1997.

Curcic, Dimitrije. "Nonfiction Book Sales Statistics." January 16, 2023. https://wordsrated.com/nonfiction-book-sales-statistics/.

Curtis, A. Kenneth, J. Stephen Lang, and Randy Petersen. *The 100 Most Important Events in Christian History*. New ed. Grand Rapids: Revell, 1998.

Davis, Glen. "Pre-Christian Uses of 'Gospel.'" *Glen Davis* (blog), February 25, 2010. https://glenandpaula.com/wordpress/archives/2010/02/25/pre-christian-uses-of-gospel.

Drane, John. *The McDonaldization of the Church: Consumer Culture and the Church's Future*. Macon, GA: Smyth & Helwys, 2012.

Dubose, Francis M. *God Who Sends: A Fresh Quest for Biblical Mission*. Nashville: Broadman Press, 1983.

BIBLIOGRAPHY

Eberhard, Arnold. *Salt and Light: Living the Sermon on the Mount*. Rifton, New York: The Plough, 1998.

Elwell, Walter A., and Philip W. Comfort. *Tyndale Bible Dictionary*. Illustrated ed. Carol Stream, IL: Tyndale House, 2008.

Every Home for Christ. *Reviving Mission: Equipping Your Church to Engage in Spiritual Conversations*. Colorado Springs, CO: Every Home for Christ, 2021.

Flynn, J. D. "Catholic Hospitals Comprise One Quarter of World's Healthcare, Council Reports." Catholic News Agency, 2010. http://www.catholicnewsagency.com/news/catholic_hospitals_represent_26_percent_of_worlds_health_facilities_reports_pontifical_council.

Fredericksen, Linwood et al. "Biblical Literature—New Testament Literature." *Encyclopædia Britannica*, online ed. https://www.britannica.com/topic/biblical-literature/New-Testament-literature.

Goff, Bob. *Everybody, Always: Becoming Love in a World Full of Setbacks and Difficult People*. Nashville: Thomas Nelson, 2018.

González, Justo L. *The Story of Christianity*. Vol. 2, *The Reformation to the Present Day*. 2nd ed. New York: HarperOne, 2014.

Green, Michael. *Evangelism through the Local Church*. Nashville: Oliver-Nelson, 1992.

Groeschel, Craig. *Winning the War in Your Mind: Change Your Thinking, Change Your Life*. Grand Rapids: Zondervan, 2021.

Harney, Kevin, and Sherry Harney. *Organic Disciples: Seven Ways to Grow Spiritually and Naturally Share Jesus*. Grand Rapids: Zondervan, 2021.

———. *Organic Outreach for Families: Turning Your Home into a Lighthouse*. Grand Rapids: Zondervan, 2012.

Hayford, Jack W. *Worship His Majesty*. Waco, TX: Word, 1987.

Hiebert, Paul G. *Transforming Worldviews: An Anthropological Understanding of How People Change*. Grand Rapids: Baker Academic, 2008.

Hybels, Bill, and Mark Mittelberg. *Becoming a Contagious Christian*. Grand Rapids: Zondervan, 1994.

Jones, Scott J. *The Evangelistic Love of God & Neighbor: A Theology of Witness and Discipleship*. Nashville: Abingdon, 2003.

Keller, Timothy. *Preaching: Communicating Faith in an Age of Skepticism*. New York: Penguin, 2015.

Kennedy, D. James. *Evangelism Explosion*. Wheaton, IL: Tyndale House, 1970.

Larsen, David L. *The Evangelism Mandate: Recovering the Centrality of Gospel Preaching*. Wheaton, IL: Crossway, 1992.

Lingenfelter, Sherwood G. *Leading Cross-Culturally: Covenant Relationships for Effective Christian Leadership*. Grand Rapids: Baker Academic, 2008.

Litfin, A. Duane. *Word versus Deed: Resetting the Scales to a Biblical Balance*. Wheaton, IL: Crossway, 2012.

Lust, Johan, Erik Eynikel, and Katrin Hauspie. *A Greek-English Lexicon of the Septuagint*. Rev. ed. Stuttgart: Deutsche Bibelgesellschaft, 2003.

Newbigin, Lesslie. *The Gospel in a Pluralist Society.* Grand Rapids: Eerdmans; Geneva: WCC, 1989.

Niles, Daniel T. *That They May Have Life.* Early New York: Harper, 1951.

Ritzer, George. *The McDonaldization of Society: Into the Digital Age.* 10th ed. Thousand Oaks, CA: SAGE, 2020.

Schaal, David. "Intentional Engagement: Toward an Evangelistic Initiative of Gospel Proclamation." PhD diss. Fuller Theological Seminary, School of Intercultural Studies, 2020.

Shelley, Marshall. "Heart & Soul." *Christianity Today*, CT Pastors. July 1, 1996. https://www.christianitytoday.com/pastors/1996/summer/6l3130.html, 1996.

Silvoso, Ed. *That None Should Perish: How to Reach Entire Cities for Christ through Prayer Evangelism.* Ventura, CA: Regal, 1994.

Soanes, Catherine, and Angus Stevenson, eds. *Concise Oxford English Dictionary.* 11 ed. Oxford: Oxford University Press, 2005.

Stanton, Glenn. "FactChecker: Misquoting Francis of Assisi." The Gospel Coalition, July 10, 2012. https://www.thegospelcoalition.org/article/factchecker-misquoting-francis-of-assisi/.

Stetzer, Ed. "Preach the Gospel, and Since It's Necessary, Use Words." *The Exchange* (blog), July 10, 2012. https://www.christianitytoday.com/edstetzer/2012/june/preach-gospel-and-since-its-necessary-use-words.html.

Stott, John. *Christian Mission in the Modern World.* Downers Grove, IL: InterVarsity , 2015.

Van Engen, Charles Edward van. *Mission on the Way: Issues in Mission Theology.* Grand Rapids: Baker, 1996.

Willard, Dallas. *The Great Omission: Reclaiming Jesus's Essential Teachings on Discipleship.* San Francisco: HarperSanFrancisco, 2006.

Wright, Christopher J. H. *The Mission of God's People: A Biblical Theology of the Church's Mission.* 1st ed. Grand Rapids: Zondervan, 2010.

Zodhiates, Spiros. *The Complete Word Study Dictionary: New Testament.* Chattanooga, TN: AMG, 2000.

www.ingramcontent.com/pod-product-compliance
Lightning Source LLC
Chambersburg PA
CBHW071434160426
43195CB00013B/1903